FORGOTTEN REVOLUTION

Limerick Soviet 1919

Described on its side as His Majesty's "Scotch and Soda", this tank guarded Wellesley (later Sarsfield) Bridge.

A military barricade during the Limerick soviet, near Thomond Bridge.

FORGOTTEN
REVOLUTION

Limerick Soviet 1919
A Threat To British Power In Ireland

LIAM CAHILL

Foreword Jim Kemmy

THE O'BRIEN PRESS
DUBLIN

First published 1990 by The O'Brien Press Ltd.,
20 Victoria Road, Dublin 6, Ireland.

British Library Cataloguing in Publication Data
Cahill, Liam
Forgotten revolution: Limerick Soviet 1919: a threat to
British power in Ireland.
1. Limerick (county), Limerick, history
I. Title
941.945
ISBN 0-86278-194-9

10 9 8 7 6 5 4 3 2 1

The author and publisher wish to thank
the following for photographs and illustrations
used in this book: Limerick Civic Museum pages 116, 142;
reproductions from *Revolt of the Bottom Dog*, Limerick Labour History
Research Group pages 65, 67, 76; the National Library of Ireland pages 86;
the National Library of Ireland Lawrence Collection pages 6 and 35, 37, 40;
George Spillane, A.I.P.F., pages 2 and 92, 33, 61, 63 and 130;
and pages 1, 107, 112, (originals from the late R. Mitchell). The
original artwork for the map of Limerick was supplied by Ian Dodson, Jr.

Cover design: The Graphiconies, Dublin
Separations: The City Office, Dublin
Typesetting: The O'Brien Press, Dublin

Printed in Great Britain by
Billing & Sons Ltd, Worcester

Contents

Limerick city centre around the time of the soviet.

Foreword

The period from 1917 to 1919 was a time of world revolutionary turmoil and stirring working-class struggles. The traumatic effect of the Bolshevik Revolution of October 1917, and the disturbed aftermath of the First World War transformed Europe into a boiling cauldron of political and industrial unrest. In 1919, a wave of revolt swept across the continent, bringing protests, strikes, insurrections and uprisings. Soviets and communes were spontaneously set up in many countries.

Ireland experienced some of the tremors of this upheaval. A combination of external and internal influences found expression in working-class activity in different parts of the country. In Limerick many workers, led by the leaders of the United Limerick Trades and Labour Council, had grown in political consciousness. This development had been sharpened by a number of events, notably the effects of the 1913 Dublin Lockout, the influence of the writings and death of James Connolly and the participation of the Citizen Army in the 1916 Rising.

This new awareness found an outlet in the appearance on 20 October 1917 of Limerick's first working-class paper, *The Bottom Dog*. This weekly publication was written and circulated by some of the leaders of the trades council and continued for at least forty-nine editions to November 1918. Labour Day was celebrated by Limerick workers for the first time on 1 May 1918, when over 10,000 workers marched through the streets. A local press report described the event: "It was a striking display of the strength and solidarity of organised labour in the city, and the appeal of the Trades and Labour Council to celebrate the day was most successful."

The demonstration ended with speeches from three platforms at the Markets' Field, where the assembled workers passed a resolution, to the sound of a trumpet. The first part of this resolution read: "That we the workers of Limerick and district, in mass meeting assembled, extend fraternal greetings to the workers of all countries, paying particular tribute to our Russian comrades who have waged such a magnificent struggle for their social and political emancipation." Thus it can be seen from the language used in the text of the resolution that the Russian Revolution had repercussions in Limerick and the expression of solidarity by the city's workers shows the extent of their developing class consciousness.

The Irish Transport and General Workers Union campaigned vigorously to organise general workers into its young Limerick branch. But other forces were also at work. The rise of Sinn Féin to political power brought another potent influence into working-class consciousness. The period 1917-1919 was remarkable for the variety and verve of the fugitive publications that appeared in the city. Broadsheets such as *The Factionist, The Irish Republic, The Soldier Hunter* and *The Republic* fanned the flames of nationalism, and used every available exhortation to hasten the destabilisation of British rule. *The Bottom Dog, The Worker* and *The Workers' Bulletin* sought to build a working-class consciousness within the broad, burgeoning nationalist movement.

All these publications had a common aim: to end British rule and to bring about a new order as soon as possible. There were, of course, differences in the concept of this order, but these differences were to be put aside when it came to the general strike in Limerick in April 1919. The strike was called by the Limerick United Trades and Labour Council as a protest against restrictions imposed by the British military authorities on people entering and leaving the city.

The Workers' Bulletin, in an article titled "The New Era", published on 8 April 1919, five days before the strike – which immediately became known as the Limerick Soviet – broke out, had no doubt but that the day of capitalist reckoning was to hand:

> Disguise it as they may, the Capitalistic Press must admit the fact that the new era is upon them. The old order – the order of repression, starvation and force – is on the brink of the precipice, and no power on earth can prevent it toppling over. For centuries that bad old order has been held up to us as the key-stone of civilisation ... but if we have learned anything we must have learned by now that the present system – no matter what name we call it by – is a system of greed and oppression ... What the workers want is to release those things that constitute capital and real wealth from the clutches of the base profiteers and financial gamblers who exploit them for their own agrandisement to the detriment of humanity as a whole, and put them at the disposal of the nation to enrich the whole people and enable the humblest to live the life that God ordained every one of His creatures should live. To end the present system of monopoly, therefore, and replace it by a system of national ownership and democratic control, is not essential in the highest interests of the working classes, but is inevitable ...

Despite the frequent use of the name of God and the invocation of the tenets of Christianity in support of the workers' cause, religion and trade union militancy were to prove incompatible during the ten-day strike.

A vignette of the strike, given by an American journalist, Ruth Russell, of the *Chicago Tribune*, in her book *What's the Matter with Ireland*, shows the strong influence of religion on the strike's activists:

> At the door of a river street house, I mounted gritty stone steps. A red-badged man opened the door part way ... I entered a badly lit room where workingmen

sat at a long black scratched table … 'Yes this is a soviet,' said John Cronin, the carpenter who was father of the baby soviet. 'Why did we form it? Why do we pit people's rule against military rule? Of course, as workers, we are against all military … You have seen how we have thrown the crank into production … The kept press is killed, but we have substituted our own paper.' He held up a small sheet which said in large letters: The Workers' bulletin issued by the Limerick Proletariat … A few of the workers' red-badged guards came to herald the approach of the workers, and then sat down outside the hall. St Munchin's chapel bell struck the Angelus. The red-badged guards rose and blessed themselves.

After the collapse of the strike, the *Irish Times*, in its edition of 26 April 1919, stated: "…The opinion is undoubtedly entertained that the early attitude of the Roman Catholic clergy in supporting the strikers was not consistently pursued … the Executive, knowing that the people would be guided by their clergy, wisely abandoned their plans …"

This statement was further reinforced by the sermon preached by Fr W. Dwane, administrator of St Michael's Church, at the 12 noon mass on Sunday, 27 April, when he said: "…neither his Lordship nor the clergy were consulted before the strike was declared, and were teetotally opposed to its continuance."

Even without the decisive intervention of the Roman Catholic bishop, Dr. Hallinan, the strike would almost certainly have petered out without massive outside support. During its ten days' duration, the military authorities maintained a calm, watchful attitude, and refused to be drawn into precipitative action. No direct concessions were made to the strikers.

For all their radical rhetoric, the strike leaders lacked a consistent and clear-cut socialist perspective. After the ending of the strike, they quickly found an accommodation within the new nationalist consensus, and never again attempted to play a leading part in the political life of the city. Without strong leadership, the rank-and-file workers became disorientated, and their militancy dissipated.

The strike was to mark the highest point in the attempt to build a socialist movement in Limerick. Recriminations and internal differences among the leaders of the local trade union movement, the rise to power of Sinn Féin, the 1922 Civil War and the pervasive influence of nationalism in the new state ensured that capitalism, and not socialism, was the driving force of future political development. Socialism evaporated in the cold, harsh dawn of the Free State, and the labour movement was relegated to the minor role of a supporting player on the political stage. After the strike, socialism was to disappear from the political agenda in Limerick, and would not re-appear until the mid-1960s, almost fifty years after the soviet.

However, the Limerick United Trades and Labour Council did not disappear; it was foremost in pressing the nationalist position within the Irish Trade Union Congress, and was the only urban trades council not to contest the 1920 local elections. Two years later, only the Limerick and Dublin trades councils opposed the labour movement's participation in the 1922 general election. In the same year, the Limerick trades council proposed a motion at the annual conference of the Irish TUC which asserted that only Irish trade unions could cater for Irish workers. The motion was attacked by a Galway delegate who stated:"We talk a lot about internationalism and we practise parochialism ... It is a green resolution from green people ."

Worse was to follow. During the Spanish Civil War, the leaders of the Limerick labour movement, political and trade union, spoke from a Christian Front platform in the city in support of General Franco. Less than two decades after the 1918 motion expressing solidarity with the Russian Revolution, the movement had come full cycle in terms of rhetoric and ideology. By this time, apart from spasmodic protests, the Irish labour movement had become badly emasculated, resulting in its almost complete political subservience to the prevailing orthodoxy.

For all its shortcomings and the anti-climax of its ending and aftermath, the Limerick Soviet was not a minor, parochial affair. Readers of Liam Cahill's book, *The Forgotten Revolution*, will find echoes and parallels in the current political upheaval in the Soviet Union and Eastern Europe. Thus the work has a topical relevance, and the lessons to be learned from the strike have a timeless and universal application.

A book on the Limerick Soviet is long overdue, and Liam Cahill has written a well-researched and balanced account of the strike and its historical context. The work fills a long-felt need in Irish labour history.

The story of the Soviet deserves to be brought to a new and wider audience. Liam Cahill has told this story fully and fairly in *The Forgotten Revolution*.

Jim Kemmy
March 1990

Acknowledgments

For many years, Jim Kemmy has been in the forefront of research and scholarship on the events of the Limerick soviet. Mere words hardly suffice to acknowledge his contribution to the research and writing of this book nor to repay the debt which I owe him. At all times, he was free with access to his invaluable trove of original materials on the soviet and to his stockpile of relevant material, both published and unpublished. More importantly, perhaps, he gave freely of his advice and experience at vital stages of the project. Without his invaluable assistance and encouragement, this book could not have been written at all.

In Chapter 3 I have relied heavily on James M Dalgleish's pioneering MA thesis for Warwick University, entitled "The Limerick Soviet", for the demographic information on Limerick. That thesis, and another on the soviet, by Timothy Molan for NIHE, Limerick, were useful cross-references for my own research.

Kevin O'Connor, a Limerickman, and a former colleague of mine in the newsroom of RTE, carried out an important interview with Charles St George of Limerick, a contemporary witness of some of the key events mentioned in the narrative. I am grateful to to them both for the trouble they took.

Joe Clarke undertook extremely important research on my behalf in London, while Michael Cannon checked archival material in Paris. At my request, Father Liam O'Sullivan made a thorough search of the Limerick diocesan archives for relevant material.

Thanks are due to the administrators and staff of several libraries and archives for their efficient and courteous assistance over several years of research: The National Library of Ireland, the State Paper Office, Dublin, the Public Record Office, London, and the British Library, Colindale.

In RTE, the librarian Maire ní Mhurchu and the library staff were cheerful and indefatigable in dealing with a variety of queries and requests for books. Tom Holton of the stills department was also of assistance.

Finally, a sincere word of thanks to my wife, Patricia, for her tolerance and patience during the lengthy period of preparation of the book.

Liam Cahill

Abbreviations

CBS – Crime Branch Special
CO – Colonial Office
CSORP – Chief Secretary's Office Registered Papers
D-I – District Inspector
I-G – Inspector General
ILPTUC – Irish Labour Party and Trade Union Congress
ITGWU – Irish Transport and General Workers' Union
LUTLC – Limerick United Trades and Labour Council
NLI – National Library of Ireland
PRO – Public Record Office, London
RIC – Royal Irish Constabulary
SPO – State Paper Office, Dublin
WO – War Office

In the case of CSORP documents, these are cited by year and by the final reference number given in the office registers for that year.

CHAPTER ONE

The Empires Crumble

"On Monday 14 April, there began in Limerick City a strike protest against military tyranny, which because of its dramatic suddenness, its completeness and the proof it offered that workers' control signifies perfect order, excited worldwide attention."
Irish Labour Party and Trade Union Congress, Annual Report 1919

On Monday, 14 April 1919, the *Irish Independent* correspondent in Limerick telegraphed the Dublin office: "Limerick City is on strike. Shops, warehouses and factories are closed. No work is being done and no business transacted."[1]

The strike had been declared by Limerick United Trades and Labour Council to protest against the proclamation of the city by the British authorities as a special military area, under the Defence of the Realm Act. The military control regulations required all citizens to carry special permits and thousands of workers faced the prospect of police scrutiny several times a day as they went to and from work. By Monday evening, 14,000 Limerick workers had joined the strike.

Within twenty-four hours, the strike committee became the effective governing body of Ireland's fourth largest city for the duration of the strike. The strike committee – or the "soviet" as it became known – regulated the price and distribution of food, published its own newspaper and printed its own currency. It was the first workers' soviet in Britain or Ireland and it brought the Irish Labour movement to the brink of a revolutionary confrontation with British power in Ireland.

The Limerick soviet was organised Labour's first – and in the event, fatally flawed – intervention in the Irish War of Independence.

The years 1917 to 1919 saw Europe in a red, revolutionary turmoil. The Bolshevik October Revolution in Russia, and the defeat of Germany and the Central European powers, had broken the old moulds with a vengeance. In an editorial on 7 April 1919, the *Irish Times* summed up the situation aptly: "The mind of the world is still torn between war and peace."[2] During that month, Europe held its breath as the old order in Germany, in particular, reeled under a succession of Bolshevik victories. At Munich, Bavaria was declared a Soviet Republic. There were general strikes or soviets in Dusseldorf, Augsburg, Würzburg and Regensburg. Thirty-eight thousand Ruhr miners went on strike, there was a general strike in the Krupps engineering company and the strike movement was said to be spreading.

The April newspapers reported that the Red Army had occupied Sebastopol, in the Crimea, as the Bolsheviks' efforts to drive the Allies out of Russia continued to meet with success. With a Hungarian Soviet Republic already in existence, a Bavarian delegate to the Berlin Soldiers' Council could hardly be faulted for boasting: " ... nothing could prevent a Red revolution ... The whole continent of Europe would become Bolshevik".[3]

Further afield, the aftermath of the Great War was bringing increasing pressure to bear on the British Empire, and fissures were beginning to appear in the imperial structure. In early 1919 Britain faced revolt in Egypt, Afghanistan and India. In the same edition of 15 April that reported the proclamation of Limerick and the ensuing general strike, *The Times* reported very grave disturbances at Amritsar, in the Punjab. An editorial laconically noted a Mr M.K.Gandhi figuring conspicuously in the reports and described him as a "misguided and excitable person".

Nearer home the great engineering cities like Glasgow and Belfast were feeling the effects of the run-down of the war machine and there were demands to reduce the resultant unemployment and create jobs for the demobilised soldiers. The unions had negotiated a forty-seven hour week, but in Belfast the workers struck for a forty-four hour week and in Glasgow they demanded a forty hour week, with no reduction in wages.

Belfast moved first and stayed out longer. There were twenty-six trade unions on the General Strike Committee, including representatives of workers in municipal transport and electricity. All factories, except those able to generate their own power, were closed but power to hospitals was maintained. Theatres and cinemas were closed and even the gravediggers went on strike! To move a ship in or out of the harbour or dry dock required permission from the strike committee. The Belfast strike involved over 40,000 workers in a loss of three-quarters of a million workdays. After almost a month on strike, and after enduring a virtual military occupation, Belfast returned to work without a victory.

The government called out the troops to deal with Glasgow. The secretary of state for Scotland described the strike as "a Bolshevist rising" and sixty tanks and 100 army lorries were sent north by rail.[4] Troops garrisoned all the major public buildings and the power stations and patrolled the streets in full battle dress. Barbed wire and machine guns surrounded the City Chambers. The show of force eventually caused a drift back to work. Later on, there were major strikes in Liverpool, Southampton, Tyneside and London.

Ireland had been experiencing something of a revolutionary ferment during those years too, though its place in the British Empire meant its revolution was political in form and content as well as social or economic. Largely through the events of the Limerick soviet, the year 1919 saw the resolution of the question of whether political issues could be separated from social or economic issues, and if they could, which should take primacy.

During the latter part of the nineteenth century and the first decade-and-a-half of the twentieth, Irish disaffection with British rule expressed itself mainly through constitutional pressure from the Irish National Party and the Land League's extra-constitutional agitation for land reform. Since the abortive Fenian risings of the 1860s, many of the Irish nationalists who favoured violence had been forced to lick their wounds and brood over past wrongs as exiles in the United States or as convicts in Britain's distant colonies. At home, Parnell's charismatic leadership and his ambivalent attitude towards the Fenians had enticed the young men towards more peaceful politics. Davitt's Land League campaign offered a potent mixture of direct action and economic aims that were attractive on an individual as well as a national level. By the outbreak of World War I, the land question had been well settled by a succession of land acts transforming the Irish peasant from a precarious tenant of an often absent landlord into a doughty land proprietor in his own right.

In politics, the Liberal government's Home Rule Bill of 1912 seemed to give just the measure of self-government needed to satisfy the demands of Ireland's "strong" farmers and business men. But Ulster and Conservative opposition, and the outbreak of World War 1, forced the postponement, until the end of hostilities, of the Irish Party's most prized achievement. In June 1916 John Redmond, the leader of the party, was forced to accept Ulster's "temporary" exclusion from the terms of the Home Rule Act, whenever it came into force. This capitulation was extremely unpopular in nationalist Ireland and, as a result, the Irish Party began to decline in popularity. The party's virtual demise in the general election of 1918 was hastened by its advocacy of Irishmen volunteering to fight in the war, by the execution of the leaders of the 1916 rising and by the death of Redmond in March 1918.

The 1916 Easter rising represented a new and more advanced phase in the Irish struggle for independence. The rising came as a great shock to a Britain lulled into a false sense of security by the majority of nationalists' apparently passive acceptance of Home Rule. On the military front, the insurgents did better than expected, though internal wrangling about strategy on the eve of the rising thinned out their numbers considerably. Coming, as it did, while the Great War was not prospering for Britain and her allies, the rebellion in the second city of the empire provoked a vehement reaction. Courts martial sentenced ninety prisoners to death and twenty-five of them were actually executed. A total of 3,500 people were arrested. More than 170 of those faced court martial while over 1,800 were interned without trial in Britain.

The execution of the leaders and the imprisonment and internment of the rank and file helped generate a growing disillusionment with British rule, with the suspended offer of Home Rule and with the moderate Irish National Party, led by John Redmond.

For over eighteen months after Easter 1916 many of the leading figures in the independence movement were out of political circulation and the stage was, largely, left free for the trade unions. In the years immediately after 1916, the upsurge of independence sentiment found its nearest and clearest expression through the Labour movement and through associated strikes and agrarian unrest.

"By the autumn and winter of 1916," an Irish Trade Union Congress report noted, " the Transport Union and Liberty Hall had begun to rise literally from their ashes ... All through the country the unions had the same tale of successful organisation and successful movements to tell in 1917 ... and indeed the two great phenomena of 1917 in Ireland were the rapid rise of Sinn Féin (the Irish Republican Party), and the equally rapid rise to both power and popularity of the militant Labour movement." [5]

James Larkin and James Connolly had founded the Irish Transport and General Workers' Union (ITGWU) in 1909. After initial successes in Belfast, Wexford, Dublin and other cities, the union had been almost bled to death by the Great Lock Out of 1913 in Dublin. By April 1916, it had a membership of only 5,000, mostly in Dublin. It was burdened with debts from the Lock Out and its headquarters had been destroyed in the rising.

The ITGWU annual report for 1918 summed up the union's progress after the rising by saying that Easter week 1916 had saved the union by cancelling out the reaction from 1913 and giving birth to the links between the Labour and nationalist movements. [6] The report noted that the ITGWU had got the full advantage of "a general zeal for Trade Unionism", stimulated by the economic conditions created by the war and the growth of a more self-reliant spirit in the country. [7] During 1918 the ITGWU nearly trebled its membership to almost 68,000. [8] Over the following eighteen months, the union signed up more than 40,000 further members. Many of them were farm labourers spurred on by the prospect of sharing in the benefits of the relatively high wartime levels of prosperity and employment in agriculture and by the erosion of earnings through price inflation. The wartime switch from pasture to the more labour-intensive tillage farming led to an increased demand for labourers, while at the same time, the supply of male labour was constrained by people joining the British army or working in munitions factories. The government recognised the upward pressure on farm wages by the establishment, in 1917, of Agricultural Wages Boards. These provided a new and more effective forum in which the ITGWU could satisfy its increasing membership with tangible results. In addition, the benevolent support of Sinn Féin and the Irish Party, both anxious to win Labour's favour, was a further factor in the union's tremendous growth.

The expansion of the ITGWU into many parts of rural Ireland not only brought extra membership, but gave the union an improved geographical spread and an improved balance between urban and rural membership. The union mopped up many of the existing small rural labourers' societies. The traditional labourer's aspiration – that of independently owning a bigger plot of land – was replaced by the more immediate aim, to be achieved by group action, of improved wages and conditions, thus creating a rural working-class. In another union publication of 1918, *Lines of Progress*, the ITGWU declared: "The days of the local society are dead; the day of the Craft Union is passing; the day for the One Big Union has come." [9] These developments gave the ITGWU a dominant role in the Irish Trade Union Congress. The union was centrally strong, and tightly organised, and the TUC's influence expanded as the Transport Union spread. By the beginning of 1918, the Labour movement had doubled its membership. [10]

In April of that year, Labour entered the forefront of the national struggle. It took its place as an equal with the declining Irish Party and the resurgent Sinn Féin in the Mansion House Conference against conscription. This position, at the centre of events, reflected Labour's greatly increased strength, influence and prestige.

Early in 1918 the British army badly needed more troops for the western front. On 21 March 1918, the Germans began a bombardment along a forty-to-fifty-mile front, with an advantage in numbers of four to one. There was a grave danger that General Ludendorff's superior forces would break through, capture Paris and cut off the Allies' lifeline of the Channel ports. The British government turned to Ireland, and conscription of the Irish, as an untapped reservoir of manpower for the battlefields. Despite opposition from the entire Irish Party, conscription for Ireland was voted through at Westminster on 18 April 1918.

That same day, acting on a resolution of Dublin Corporation, the lord mayor of Dublin, Lawrence O'Neill, convened a conference or "national cabinet" at the Mansion House to "formulate a national policy to defeat this menace" of conscription. Three representatives of the Irish Trade Union Congress and Labour Party – William O'Brien, Thomas Johnson and Michael Egan – took their places along with national figures like Eamon de Valera and Arthur Griffith for Sinn Féin and John Dillon and Timothy Healy for the Irish Parliamentary Party.

The conference issued an anti-conscription pledge and declaration. The pledge promised to use "all the means that may be deemed effective" to resist compulsory military service and the declaration regarded the passing of the Conscription Bill as a declaration of war on the Irish nation. [11] That same evening the Catholic bishops, who were holding their annual meeting at Maynooth, met a delegation from the conference. The bishops said that conscription, forced on Ireland against its will and against the protests of its leaders, was an oppressive and inhuman law, which the Irish people had the right to resist by every means consonant with the law of God. [12]

Throughout nationalist Ireland the pledge was signed by tens of thousands, often outside Catholic church gates. Despite a ban by the authorities, a substantial national defence fund was built up.

But Labour made its own distinctive contribution to the anti-conscription campaign. Fifteen hundred delegates attended an Extraordinary Labour Conference in Dublin and "amid scenes of indescribable enthusiasm" called for a general strike on 23 April 1918 in protest at the government's proposal. [13] The call was responded to everywhere except in the Unionist areas of north-east Ulster. Railways, docks, factories, mills, theatres, cinemas, trams, public services, shipyards, newspapers, shops, even government munitions factories all stopped. The strike was described as "complete and entire, an unprecedented event outside the continental countries". [14] It was, in fact, the first general strike in any country against measures for greater participation in the Great War.

The *Irish Times* commented that 23 April would be "chiefly remembered as the day on which Irish Labour realised its strength". [15] The Irish TUC strike declaration stressed the claim to "independent status as a nation and the right of self-determination". [16] But it also contained a call to workers in other countries involved in the war to emulate Ireland's example and "rise against their oppressors and bring the war to an end". [17] The day after the strike, the Irish TUC conveyed the international message in a Manifesto to the Organised Workers of England and Wales. The manifesto said Irish Labour was resolutely against conscription for any war, whether imposed by a British, an Irish or any other authority. [18] The British Labour movement responded with an appeal to their government not to enforce conscription in Ireland, mainly because of the appalling consequences for both countries that would ensue.

In the summer of 1918, the Labour members of the anti-conscription conference put forward a plan for the further use of strikes in the campaign which was adopted formally by the conference in October 1918. [19] The trade union plan was to swing the entire country behind the area in which the terms of the Military Service Act were first imposed. If martial law was imposed and permits became necessary, special anti-conscription organisations, based on the military areas, would be set up. The unions' "plan of campaign" included the calling of a railway strike for a limited period and a general stoppage. All civil servants, including the constabulary, were to be urged to join in the downing of tools.

A trade union memorandum on the campaign considered the possibility of calling a general strike in Dublin. It would last one week, and would be a massive demonstration of passive resistance. Food supplies would have to be maintained and it was hoped sympathetic farmers in Co. Dublin would help out. Inside the city, there would be a central committee to organise rationing and food distribution.

The government eventually withdrew its threat of conscription so the trade union plan never had to be put into action. However, the plan for a general strike in Dublin bore a close resemblance to what actually happened later in Limerick.

By August 1918 the press censor was reporting that Labour had replaced Sinn Féin as the leaders in the fight against conscription. He regarded the development of the Irish TUC since April as the most noteworthy aspect of the previous few months. A British cabinet report noted that Labour and Sinn Féin "were now working together and had come to an arrangement." [20]

Not everyone in the all-class nationalist alliance against conscription was pleased at the Mansion House conference's public endorsement of Labour's predominant role. Senior influential elements of Sinn Féin were unhappy because they recognised that "direct action", such as strikes, would be outside their control and would give too much influence to the trade unions in determining the outcome of the struggle. People like Arthur Griffith, the founder of Sinn Féin, ostensibly did not want to foster any trends that might disrupt the all-class unity of the national movement, but equally they did not foresee a dominant role for Labour in their vision of a free Ireland. In January 1919 Griffith wrote: "The general strike is a weapon that might injure as much as serve. It would be injudicious at present and might be injudicious at any time, unless under extreme circumstances ... " [21]

From another perspective, in the same month, another observer noted the growing rivalry between Sinn Féin and Labour for pre-eminence. In his monthly report for January 1919, the inspector-general of the Royal Irish Constabulary (RIC), Joseph Aloysius Byrne, remarked that he saw Labour sooner or later becoming a formidable rival to Sinn Féin. [22]

Towards the end of 1918, the only check to Labour's advance was its decision, under Sinn Féin persuasion and pressure, not to contest the December general election. Sinn Féin wanted to ensure that the election in Ireland was fought on the simple issue of self-determination, uncluttered by any social issues.

The original, unanimous decision of the Labour executive had been to contest a number of seats. The Waterford annual congress, in August 1918, had called for the setting up of Labour electoral machinery in every municipal and parliamentary constituency where this was found practicable. Conscious that the new franchise laws would greatly increase the electoral register, local Labour organisations were given a four-point plan of action to maximise their vote.

The Labour congress decision to contest was based on three grounds: to give workers an opportunity to vote Labour, to strengthen the Irish movement's standing with the Socialist International and to prepare the way for full Labour representation in any future Irish parliament. But, in a concession to the Sinn Féin view, elected Labour members would not take their seats at Westminster unless an annual or special congress decided otherwise.

Labour in Dublin made an early decision to contest four seats. Elsewhere, there was confusion and indeed opposition to the executive's decision – in places like Meath, Bray, Cork, Waterford and Kilkenny. At a meeting of forty-three rail workers in Kingstown, Co. Dublin, only six were prepared to vote Labour. The rest thought it better to have a straight fight between Sinn Féin and the Irish National Party solely on the issue of self-determination. At election rallies, Labour speakers came under increasing pressure.

Nationally there were confidential but inconclusive negotiations between Sinn Féin and Labour to see if a compromise could be found. Some Sinn Féin leaders feared that if there was no agreement, while Labour would not win any seats, they might prevent Sinn Féin winning in up to twenty constituencies.

On 1 November 1918 the congress executive returned to the question of the election. The congress treasurer Tom Johnson, who initiated the discussion, pointed out that great changes had taken place since the first decision and said it was desirable to review the whole position in the light of the new circumstances. At a special congress that day, Johnson argued that they had originally envisaged the election as a "war" election, but it had now become a "peace" election. With the possibility of new national boundaries being drawn elsewhere, Labour in Ireland should withdraw to allow a demonstration of unity on the question of self-determination.

Cathal O'Shannon, of the ITGWU, was against any change in electoral strategy. He said they would not get full representation at the Socialist International unless they had a parliamentary Labour Party. They were cutting away one-third of their numerical representation and one-half of their moral strength. But, many delegates reported a determination at local level to vote Sinn Féin and the national executive's change of policy was endorsed by ninety-six votes to twenty-three.

The desire to give Sinn Féin a "clear run" on the issue of self-determination was obviously a major factor in Labour's decision. Equally, the national leadership could hardly impose a policy of electoral participation in the teeth of widespread local determination to support Sinn Féin. That would have led to a damaging confrontation with an increasingly confident and united Sinn Féin. In addition, because of the nature of its organisation and the looser degree of adherence of its members, Labour did not have the same organisational or electoral coherence as Sinn Féin. The latter had a highly politicised organisation and its members were strongly under the influence or control of its leaders. Labour, on the other hand, was made up of people who might be staunch trade unionists in industrial matters but were often pledged supporters of Sinn Féin when it came to politics.

In the minds of some Labour leaders there was another factor – the North. It would have been relatively easy to have reached a pact with Sinn Féin on the contesting of seats, but how would that have been viewed by the Loyalist trade unionists of Ulster? The dilemma of trying to reconcile a united trade union centre, North and South, with the conflicting nationalist aspirations of the rank-and-file membership paralysed the leadership and was at the root of its political impotence.

Finally, Labour's commitment to syndicalist policies may have been a residual influence in restraining the movement from engaging in electoral or parliamentary politics. In a sense it could be argued that the abstention decision freed attention and resources to concentrate on the industrial issues at hand.

Nevertheless, Labour's decision not to contest the 1918 general election is regarded by many, especially on the left, as the starting point of the left's subsequent historical weakness. An analysis of the electoral register for that election shows the potential there was for advance. Among many reforms, the Representation of the People Act 1918 provided a vote on a simple basis of age and residence in a constituency. The system of plural voting, loaded in favour of property owners, was abolished. In Ireland, the result was a dramatic restructuring and increase in the electorate. The number of voters in the major cities was trebled, providing fertile ground for Labour progress.

Conscious of the international recognition it might bring, Sinn Féin and the Volunteers had to maintain close and friendly ties with Labour. In February 1919, Thomas Johnson and Cathal O'Shannon represented the Irish Trade Union Congress at the International Socialist conference in Berne called by Socialist and Labour leaders to consider the post-war situation. In a major boost to independence sentiment, Johnson and O'Shannon succeeded in getting Ireland recognised, and seated, as a separate delegation to the conference.

At Berne, the Irish delegates presented a special report to the International outlining the case for Irish independence. This was prepared in Irish, English, French and German. A further memorandum was issued in French and German sketching Irish history, reviewing the current situation and expressing working-class and nationalist aspirations. The memorandum was intended to brief the representatives of the Labour International who were to attend the Paris peace conference.

At Amsterdam in April 1919 the principles of national independence and self-determination, agreed at Berne, were applied to Ireland. A resolution, adopted unanimously, demanded that the principle of free and absolute self-determination be applied to Ireland. It affirmed the right of the Irish people to political independence and required that "self-determination should rest on a democratic decision expressed by the free, equal, adult and secret vote of the people without any military, political or economic pressure from outside, or any reservation or restriction imposed by any government". [23] The International called on the Great Powers and the peace conference to "make good this rightful claim of the Irish people".

The rapid growth and negotiating successes of the trade unions, and their emphasis on industrial action over politics, intensified in 1919. In February, for example, a special conference was held in the Mansion House to initiate a national wages and hours movement – for a forty-four hour week, a 150 percent increase in pay and a minimum adult wage of fifty shillings a week. The conference was attended by delegates representing more than a hundred unions. Early in April, the executive of the Irish Transport and General Workers' Union completed a two-day session reviewing the union's activity. [24] Since the beginning of the year, there had been an increase of 79 new branches, making a total of 289. Total membership was now 85,000 – an increase of 9,000 in just over three months! The executive decided on an extensive campaign of organisation and increased by five the existing complement of seventeen organisers.

The Drapers' Assistants' Association held their annual meeting in the City Hall, in Dublin, on Easter Sunday, 22 April 1919. According to newspaper reports, "an optimistic and cheerful note pervaded the reports and speeches" and delegates were told association membership was a thousand stronger than in the best year previously recorded. [25] Again underlining the growth in trade unionism, the meeting heard that £60,000 had been secured in bonuses during the previous year and £140,000 in permanent salary increases.

In his presidential address to the Sinn Féin *Ard Fheis*, held in the Mansion House during the week beginning 7 April 1919, Eamon de Valera made it clear that he understood the essential importance of Labour's role in the independence movement: "When we wanted the help of Labour against conscription, Labour gave it to us [cheers]. When we wanted the help of Labour in Berne, Labour gave it to us and got Ireland recognised as a distinct nation [cheers]. When we wanted Labour to stand down at the election, and not divide us, but that we should stand forsworn against the enemy, Labour fell in with us. I say Labour deserves well of the Irish people: the Labour man deserves the best the country can give [cheers]." [26]

CHAPTER 2

Connolly's Legacy

"Should it come to a test in Ireland ... between those who stood for the
Irish nation and those who stood for foreign rule, the greatest civil asset in
the hand of the Irish nation for use in the struggle would be the control of
the Irish docks, shipping, railways and production by unions
that gave sole allegiance to Ireland."
James Connolly, The Workers' Republic,
January 22, 1916

Dublin Castle was not unaware of the close link – indeed, often the overlapping
of membership – between the trade unions and Sinn Féin. Through the eyes and
ears of its police force, the Royal Irish Constabulary (RIC), the British administration kept a close watch on trade union activities. Monthly reports to Dublin
from county inspectors regularly listed the ITGWU among the eleven "political"
organisations monitored for number of branches, membership and level of
activity. This put the union under the same degree of suspicion as organisations
like Sinn Féin, the Volunteers, the Gaelic Athletic Association and the Irish
language movement, the Gaelic League.

In his annual report for 1918, the inspector general of the Royal Irish
Constabulary, Joseph Byrne, commented that the Irish Transport and General
Workers' Union represented the "Socialist and Labour wing of the Irish revolutionary movement". [1] Byrne noted that in March there had been widespread
political unrest, which showed no sign of abatement. Trade was good, he noted,
but the inflation caused by war prices continued to rise and was leading to Labour
discontent.

Byrne also reported that Labour organisation was of comparatively recent
growth, but the ITGWU had spread its branches everywhere and all classes of
people were enrolled in it. He recorded strikes in eighteen counties, with nearly
all the strikers belonging to the labouring class and demanding wages of forty
to fifty shillings a week. There were few large employers in country districts and
such wages would be impossible to meet in many cases. At the same time, Byrne
conceded, the high prices charged by farmers and shopkeepers during the war

made the demand seem less unreasonable than it looked.

In March 1919, the month before the Limerick strike, Inspector-General Byrne sent a report marked "secret" and "urgent" to the chief secretary for Ireland, Ian McPherson MP. It warned that, in the prevailing discontent, if the "extremists" decided to take independent action they could "rely to a considerable extent" on the co-operation of Labour organisations and "they would certainly find a large body of fanatical Irish volunteers through the country, ready to do their bidding". [2] "Ireland", the inspector-general warned, "is unquestionably in a highly inflammable condition, and in my opinion at no time was there more urgent necessity for the presence of an overpowering military force."

The Castle's worries about Labour involvement in the independence movement were well-founded. James Connolly, the commandant-general of the 1916 rising, was a founder of the ITGWU. Apart from the practical example of his life and death, Connolly had left behind a body of political writings that strongly influenced trade union aims and the methods to be used in attaining those aims.

Many Labour people, apart from Connolly, had been prominent in the rising, many more were active in Gaelic cultural bodies and activities like the Gaelic League or the Gaelic Athletic Association. Like many others, they were profoundly affected by the aftermath of the Easter rising.

Under Connolly's influence, Irish Labour and trade unionism was strongly syndicalist in its policies and attitudes. In simple terms, syndicalism was a left-wing philosophy that stressed a connection between workers' industrial strength, exercised through trade unions, and the political struggle for the achievement of socialism. Syndicalism found its earliest organised expression in France, as a reaction to the failure of reformist, socialist political leaders to make gains commensurate with their voting strength in parliament. James Connolly had been particularly influenced by this analysis during his spell in the United States where he encountered it as an organiser for the pre-eminently syndicalist trade union, the Industrial Workers of the World.

According to syndicalist theory, workers' industrial muscle would underpin political advances, using major strikes in pursuit of political aims. Ultimately, a general strike would paralyse the existing capitalist system and result in the workers taking over the state. The workers' industrial organisations, the trade unions, would then form the basis for governing the new commonwealth.

Connolly's unique application of syndicalism to Irish conditions was to argue that the struggle for socialism and for national independence from Britain were inseparable. "The cause of Ireland is the cause of Labour, and the cause of Labour is the cause of Ireland," he wrote. [3] In his view, trade union power could therefore properly be harnessed to further the aim of independence. In the *Irish Worker* of 30 May 1914, Connolly tersely stated his view of the link between syndicalism and nationalism: "We believe that there are no real nationalists in Ireland outside the Irish Labour movement. All others merely reject one part or another of the British conquest – the Labour movement alone rejects it in its entirety and sets itself to the re-conquest of Ireland as its aim." [4]

In the foreword to his monumental work *Labour in Irish History*, Connolly linked progress in the achievement of the liberty of a subject nation with the liberty of the nation's most subject class. It was a distortion of Irish history, he argued, to deny the "relation between the social rights of the Irish toilers and the political rights of the Irish nation". [5] The basic argument of that book was that, throughout history, the better off and wealthy classes always reached an accommodation with Britain. The book's celebrated and succinct conclusion was that " ... only the Irish working-class remain as the incorruptible inheritors of the fight for freedom in Ireland".

For Connolly, the creation of a nation state was a necessary precondition, or part of, the achievement of democratic power. Irish representative bodies would reflect the popular will more accurately than similar bodies based in Britain. Only in such an Irish republic, he argued, could the battle-lines of class antagonisms, hitherto obscured by "patriotism", be clearly drawn. Thus, he reasoned, a Socialist-Republican reached the same conclusion as the "most irreconcilable Nationalist": the links with Britain must be broken. Connolly, therefore, saw Irish nationalism as the essential foundation for social and economic progress and the Irish revolution would have to be not only nationalist, but socialist as well. The Irish Trade Union Congress's plan for major strikes against conscription in 1918 was a clear expression of this fusion of political aims with trade union organisation and methods.

In January 1916, Connolly wrote in the newspaper *The Workers' Republic*: "Should it come to a test in Ireland ... between those who stood for the Irish nation and those who stood for foreign rule, the greatest civil asset in the hand of the Irish nation for use in the struggle would be the control of the Irish docks, shipping, railways and production by unions that gave sole allegiance to Ireland". [6] Here, clearly stated, was his synthesis of classical syndicalism and nationalism.

Those words of Connolly were published very shortly after he had spent three days in a secret meeting with the Irish Republican Brotherhood (IRB), being briefed on their plans for a rising. Connolly had developed close personal ties with leaders of the separatist Volunteers, like Pearse, MacDonagh, Clarke and MacDermott. In the *Workers' Republic*, he strongly advocated an insurrection and published articles on revolutionary warfare in other countries. He was severely critical of the dilatory attitude of the Volunteer leadership, something they resented greatly.

After hearing the IRB plans for an early insurrection, to take advantage of Britain's difficulties in the Great war, Connolly agreed to make available the forces of the workers' Citizen Army. He was appointed commandant-general of the Dublin forces and became a member of the Brotherhood's military council. On Easter Monday 1916, the council's seven members were declared to be the provisional government of the Irish Republic. Indeed, the proclamation of the Republic was printed in the basement of Liberty Hall, the ITGWU headquarters, under an armed guard of the Citizen Army.

The Irish Citizen Army was born out of the struggle of the Great Dublin Lock Out of 1913 to defend workers from police attacks. In March 1914 the army was reorganised and adopted its first constitution. The constitution claimed the ownership of Ireland for the people of Ireland. It stood for what it termed the "absolute unity of Irish nationhood" and for the "rights and liberties of the democracies of all nations". [7]

Every member of the army had to be a member of a trade union recognised by the Irish TUC and its declared object was to "sink all differences of birth, property and creed under the common name of Irish people". The Dublin trades council approved the new army early in April 1914, and in June a contingent led by James Larkin marched in a republican demonstration at the grave in Bodenstown of the father of Irish republicanism, Wolfe Tone.

Connolly's analysis was jealously guarded by his disciple and successor as general secretary of the ITGWU, William O'Brien, notably in his presidential address to the 1918 Trade Union Congress in Waterford. In 1918, as well, the combined party/congress adopted a new name – the Irish Labour Party and Trade Union Congress (ILPTUC) – and a new constitution that underlined its formal commitment at least, to syndicalist thinking. Article 2(c) of the new constitution pledged to secure "the democratic management and control of all industries and services by the whole body of workers, manual and mental, engaged therein..."[8]

While the Labour "wing" of the national movement prospered, the political element was enjoying success too. In the general election of December 1918 to the Westminster Parliament, Labour stood to one side. Seventy-three Irish constituencies – out of 105 – returned Sinn Féin members of parliament, committed to an independent Irish Republic. Twenty-six Unionists were returned and six members of the Irish National Party, though four of those were returned as a result of a pre-election pact with Sinn Féin in some Ulster constituencies. In votes, Sinn Féin won more than 485,000 against slightly over 277,000 for the Irish Party.

The foundation of Sinn Féin by Arthur Griffith, in 1905, was a development of a new kind of nationalism in Ireland. Since 1870, leaders of Irish nationalism had assumed the validity of the Act of Union of Great Britain and Ireland and had organised their strategy and tactics largely within the framework of the Westminster Parliament. Sinn Féin, instead, advocated that the elected members for Ireland should assemble in Dublin and initiate a national programme of economic and social reform. The essence of that programme was to be Irish economic self-reliance and political self-determination – summed up in the movement's name: *Sinn Féin*, "Ourselves Alone". Instead of taking their seats in London, then, the Sinn Féin MPs set up a separatist Republican parliament – Dáil Eireann – in Dublin on 21 January 1919. Out of the seventy-three members elected, only twenty-six could attend the opening session – the rest were in jail.

In the December 1918 general election, the British electorate had endorsed a measure of Home Rule for Ireland and with that had tried to put Irish affairs to the back of their mind. War weary as they were, the establishment of the Dáil caused barely a ripple in Britain. The *Times* Irish correspondent scoffed at what he termed the "stage play at the Mansion House", where earlier that morning there had been a "blaze of Union Jacks" at a luncheon to welcome home 400 repatriated prisoners of war, members of the Royal Dublin Fusiliers. [9] Few in Britain heeded the *Daily News* warning that it was "very easy to laugh at the Sinn Féin parliament, but it is not so certain that it is wise". [10]

The establishment of a secessionist parliament was a sophisticated development in the tactics of the independence movement. The Dáil combined the new ideas of civil resistance with the old ideal of physical rebellion. The Dáil's Address to the Free Nations of the World declared that "a state of war existed", that could not end "until Ireland is definitely evacuated by the armed forces of England". [11] This was effectively a declaration of war and it assumed more propaganda importance later, when it was looked to as the source of democratic backing for the armed struggle against Britain.

The Democratic Programme of the First Dáil Eireann – its statement of political and economic aspirations – was left-wing in tone, again reflecting the strength of Labour's position at the time. Prior to the first meeting of the Dáil, there were contacts between prominent Dáil members and Labour leaders with a view to drafting some sort of social programme.

It is clear from the exhaustively kept diary of the Labour leader William O'Brien that Labour's entitlement to representation at Berne loomed large in the background contacts on the Democratic Programme. On New Year's Day 1919, O'Brien met Richard Mulcahy, the Dáil member who later formally proposed the adoption of the programme and they discussed the Berne Socialist conference. Within a fortnight, there were two other meetings of Labour and Sinn Féin leaders at which Berne and the forthcoming opening of the Dáil were discussed. At the second of these meetings, it appears the Labour leaders submitted a document and a Dáil committee was set up to draft a social programme in consultation with Labour. On the Labour side, Tom Johnson was involved in drafting and the key person on the Dáil side was Harry Boland, a regular contact between Sinn Féin and Labour. According to Sean T. O'Kelly, a key organiser of the Dáil's proposed public sitting, Boland arrived on the night before the ceremonial opening with only a bundle of rough notes, received from Labour friends like Johnson and William O'Brien. The content of the notes aroused fierce controversy. Close to midnight, O'Kelly says he was given a free hand to draft the programme as he alone wished and he worked through the night to have it ready for the following day.

O'Kelly's final draft omitted references to eliminating "the class in society which lives upon the wealth produced by the workers of the nation but gives no useful social service in return ... " [12] Nevertheless, the Democratic Programme, in its final form, was far from being a total reflection of Sinn Féin's rather conservative economic and social thinking. It declared that the nation's sovereignty extended to all its material possessions, its soil and resources, all its wealth and wealth-producing processes. The right of private property was subordinate to the public right and, in return for willing service, every citizen had a right to an adequate share of the produce of the nation's labour. It was to be the government's first duty to provide for the physical, mental and spiritual well-being of children, "to ensure that no child shall suffer hunger or cold from lack of food, clothing or shelter, that all shall be provided with ample means and facilities requisite for the education and training of free citizens of a free nation". [13]

The main purpose of adopting the programme seems to have been to strengthen Labour's hand in seeking full representation at Berne. Labour could argue that although they did not hold parliamentary seats, the new separatist assembly was committed to a broadly socialist programme. In turn, as later events proved, the Dáil could anticipate recognition for the Irish claim to self-determination from an important international forum. And there may have been a belief in some Sinn Féin and IRB circles that Labour should receive a tangible political reward for standing aside in the election that, effectively, produced the first Dáil. To an extent, Labour's eventual refusal to participate in the December 1918 general election reflected its espousal of industrial over parliamentary methods of action. Indeed, the refusal served to reinforce its predisposition towards syndicalist methods. From beginning to end, the year 1919 saw a wave of Labour militancy wash over Ireland from North to South. Apart from the great Belfast strike of January 1919, there were strikes early in the year by building workers in Limerick, shipyard workers in Derry, asylum workers in Monaghan and strikes by farm labourers in counties Kildare, Meath and Tipperary – sometimes involving violent clashes with the police and non-union labourers.

Thus, with the formal opening of Dáil Eireann on January 21, the year began with the lines of battle more clearly drawn than at any time previously. Home Rule was gone from the agenda, the only remaining item was a republic. At the same time, violence was emerging more strongly as a tactic. On the day the Dáil formally met for the first time, IRA members attacked and killed two members of the RIC at Soloheadbeg, in Co. Tipperary. By early 1919 the leader of the attack, Dan Breen, had no doubt what form the coming struggle should take. Breen believed political campaigns, notably the general election of 1918, had "softened" many Republicans. "Many had ceased to be soldiers and had become politicians. There was a danger of disintegration, a danger which had been growing since the threat of conscription disappeared a few months earlier. I was convinced that some sort of action was absolutely necessary". [14]

On 31 January 1919 violence was given added impetus by a directive issued in the Volunteer paper, *An tOglach* (The Volunteer). The Volunteers were reminded of the Dáil's declaration of a state of war to last until there was a British military evacuation of Ireland. That state of war justified the Volunteers in treating the police and army as invaders. The authority of the nation was behind them, the editorial declared, embodied in the lawfully constituted authority of the Dáil. The Dáil, it continued, was not just a group of "militarists" or "extremists" but "the accredited representatives of the Irish people met in solemn session". Every Volunteer, it concluded, had the legal and moral right to use "all legitimate methods of warfare" against the army and police. From the end of January 1919, attacks on the RIC and British army throughout the country increased in frequency and ferocity. By the end of the year, fourteen policemen and soldiers had been killed in attacks.

Dan Breen's worries reflected the concern of Michael Collins, now adjutant general and director of organisation of the revived and rapidly growing Volunteers. All through 1918, Collins had complained that Sinn Féin seemed to lack "direction" and that those who "ought to" have been "directing" were too "lax" and did not spend enough time at the party's headquarters, No. 6, Harcourt Street in Dublin. This, despite the fact that in October 1917, the two bodies had been brought closer by the election as president of Sinn Féin of the man who was already leader of the Volunteers, Eamon de Valera.

In September 1918, *An tOglach* had grimly predicted the abandonment of political methods and passive resistance. By May 1919 Collins was complaining of an intolerable position in which the policy seemed to be to "squeeze out anyone who was tainted with strong fighting ideas". From June 1919 onwards, Collins intensified his military campaign, especially against the British detective and intelligence agencies in Dublin. By August of that year, the Dáil had passed a resolution insisting that the IRA take a formal oath of allegiance to "the Irish Republic and the Dáil".

The increasingly widespread sympathy with the separatist aim might never have developed to the extent it did, but for the attitude of the British Government in the years after the 1916 rising. This has been aptly described as one of "mild coercion – repression too weak to root out opposition, but provocative enough to nurture it". [15] After the 1916 rising, the changes in the British administration in Ireland were ones of personnel rather than structure. Martial law was imposed for a few months, but in November 1916, the commander in chief for Ireland, General Sir John Maxwell, was recalled to Britain and replaced.

The police force was split between the Dublin Metropolitan Police and, for the rest of the country, the Royal Irish Constabulary. At one time, counting military services, there were no less than seven independent intelligence services operating, with varying degrees of effectiveness. By 1917 the RIC was short 1,400 members on its original number of over 10,700 and morale was low.

After the simultaneous enactment and suspension of the Home Rule Act in September 1918, the British government's efforts to resolve its Irish political problems were spasmodic and half-hearted. They were motivated more by the aim of eliminating any problems at Britain's backdoor and thus freeing resources for the war, than by any desire to respond to the increasing Irish nationalist clamour.

Within weeks of the 1916 rising, the prime minister, Asquith, asked his then minister of munitions, Lloyd George, to initiate fresh negotiations with the leaders of Irish opinion – John Redmond for the Nationalists and Sir Edward Carson for the Ulster Unionists. Lloyd George managed to get Redmond to agree to the temporary exclusion of Ulster's six north-eastern counties from a Home Rule parliament that would govern the rest of Ireland. Unionist members of the cabinet, fearing that all of Ulster might eventually be brought in under the proposed Dublin parliament, torpedoed this plan from within the cabinet.

By May 1917, Lloyd George had become prime minister and he offered Redmond two alternative proposals to settle the Irish question. One was the application of the 1914 Home Rule Act, but with a five year exclusion of Loyalist Ulster. The second was an Irish Convention, representing all shades of opinion, which would devise a scheme of self-government. Redmond accepted the second option and the convention began its deliberations in July 1917.

Sinn Féin's refusal to attend the convention rendered it an unrepresentative talking-shop. It sat until May 1918 and produced a report in which there was little substantial agreement between the participants.

In March 1918, Field-Marshal Viscount French was appointed lord lieutenant with a mandate to enforce conscription and get tougher with separatism. On 17 May the majority of Sinn Féin leaders were taken in a series of mass arrests, but this served only to increase the influence of the militarist-orientated hard-liners in Sinn Féin.

On the very last day of 1918, a member of the British cabinet, Walter Long, secretary of state for the colonies, wrote this perceptive summary of how matters stood: "I have watched the rise and fall of every political party in Ireland for the last forty years, and I think that the present movement is much the most difficult and dangerous of any the Government has had to deal with and for this reason. Their leaders are brave and fanatical and do not fear imprisonment or death; they are not to be influenced by private negotiations with Bishops or Priests, or captured by getting the patronage of appointments, which has been the favourite instrument of the Irish Government since 1905. Neither do they care a straw for the press. It is a fair and square fight between the Irish Government and Sinn Féin as to who is going to govern the country." [16]

On 10 January 1919, French was replaced as lord lieutenant by the Liberal Scot, Ian MacPherson. MacPherson favoured Home Rule for Ireland and initially he made some conciliatory moves. However he was soon shocked into a stronger "law and order" stance by the rising tide of violence.

Limerick was far from immune to these national developments, trends and influences. Indeed, as a major city with a strong tradition of nationalism and trade unionism, it was at the forefront of events.

CHAPTER 3

Limerick, a Defiant City

" … with the exception of Londonderry, there is perhaps no other town in
Ireland in which its history bulks so large as it does in Limerick."
The Times, 17 March 1913

The Vikings founded the city and port of Limerick on the Shannon in the ninth
century. The city became a legend in Irish history with Patrick Sarsfield's
Jacobite defence of the walls in 1691 against the siege of the Orange King
William. The Treaty Stone, where by tradition the subsequent Treaty of Limerick
was signed, still stands as a monument near the Shannon.

A *Times* special supplement on Ireland, published on St Patrick's Day 1913,
caught the flavour of Limerick exactly when it said: " … with the exception of
Londonderry, there is perhaps no other town in Ireland in which its history still
bulks so large as it does in Limerick". [1]

The city had a strong tradition of Fenianism, personified by the Fenian leader
John Daly who was elected a member of parliament in the 1890s and was mayor
from 1899 to 1901. In 1867, 5,000 people marched in memory of the Manchester
martyrs, Allen, Larkin and O'Brien. With the one-time leader of the Irish
National Party, Isaac Butt, as a previous MP, Limerick was also strongly imbued
with the constitutional nationalist tradition. But in Limerick, as elsewhere in
Parnell's time, the dividing line between the two policies was often hazy.

Limerick was affected too by the Gaelic cultural renaissance that was emerging towards the end of the nineteenth century. In 1887, three years after the
foundation of the Gaelic Athletic Association, a club was established in Limerick. That year, the Limerick Commercials' Club won the first All Ireland final
in Gaelic football. A branch of the Irish language revival organisation, the Gaelic
League, was formed in Limerick in 1898, five years after its national foundation.

A year earlier, during Queen Victoria's Jubilee, the most important anti-
Royalist demonstrations were in Limerick. A black flag of protest flew from
John Daly's house and another was suspended across the river at Thomondgate.

The Irish Volunteers, founded in 1913, established a Limerick branch in
December of that year and at the time of the split over World War I, nearly 7,000

A contemporary postcard of Limerick showing the Treaty Stone, Thomond Bridge and King John's Castle.

members followed John Redmond into the National Volunteers, while 500 remained as Irish Volunteers. Limerick had a close enough connection too with the 1916 rising. Two of those executed were born in Limerick – Edward Daly, and Con Colbert – while a third, Sean Heuston, had worked there for a number of years.

Prior to the great famines of the 1840s, Limerick had a population of over 60,000 but starvation and emigration forced that down to less than 40,000. Between the end of the nineteenth century and the census of 1911, the population recovered slowly, to almost 40,000 people – making Limerick Ireland's fourth largest city. The city's economy was disproportionately dominated by industries engaged in food processing: Cleeves' Creamery, four large bacon curing factories and distilling. Apart from those, the only other major employers were the Limerick Clothing Company and O'Callaghan's Leather Factory.

World War I brought higher prices and increased prosperity to Ireland's farmers. In turn, that meant increased wealth for the thousands of pig-buyers and cattle-dealers who acted as middle men in the booming trade of exporting live animals to feed Britain's citizens and armed forces. Bankers' deposits and profits were boosted by farmers' savings and retailers too grew wealthy from farm spending.

But the composition of Limerick's industry meant that the city derived little direct economic benefit from war work. Since before the war, the Clothing Company had been getting military contracts, but there were no major engineering or munitions works that would have allowed the city to really cash in on the war effort. Irish munitions works always stood in danger from extremist raids. There were also the additional costs and U-boat hazards of the sea journey to Britain. Eventually, after much local agitation, Limerick got a small share of the munitions work done in Ireland. Overall, though, there was little reason for the government to give additional war contracts to Limerick firms, despite the frequent pleas of the city's business community.

The war also dealt a heavy blow to Limerick port. The city's geographical location, facing westwards to the Atlantic, meant that sea journeys were longer and more hazardous than from ports on the east coast. Strategic and economic reasons dictated a transfer to ports that were nearer to Britain and faced the shorter journeys and relatively safer waters of the Irish Sea. The result was a calamitous decline in traffic through Limerick port.

In 1913, 454 vessels, carrying 190,000 tons of cargo, used the port. In every succeeding year, the figures for vessels and cargo declined sharply. By 1918, the number of vessels was down to only sixty-eight and the tonnage was less than one-third of pre-war levels. The first recovery in the number of vessels and tonnage through Limerick did not occur until after the war, in 1919. The shift from west to east coast ports is also illustrated by dramatic increases in imports

The commercial heart of Limerick in years preceding the soviet. Carts like those shown had to display transport permits issued by the soviet.

of coal into Belfast and Dublin in the first two years of the war and by a dramatic decline in imports into Limerick.

Limerick port might have faced problems anyway. In 1916 the coal importers estimated that a 600-700 ton ship could be unloaded in Belfast in five to seven hours or in Cork in ten to twelve hours, but it took two to three days in Limerick. The employers blamed the dock labourers and their union for this state of affairs.

But the port was under-capitalised and unmechanised. There was no rail extension to the docks, nor were there any cranes. Throughout the war years, the dockers fought a rearguard action against the introduction of mechanisation in a vain effort to arrest a declining number of jobs. By 1917 they had reached agreement on the introduction of cranes with buckets, but when the employers tried to introduce "grab" cranes early in 1918, these were dumped in the Shannon.

The overall poor economic conditions in the city, even in the war years, meant lives of abject poverty and misery for many Limerick people. In 1916 a local priest claimed that nearly forty percent of the population lived in one or two rooms, ten times the proportion in Belfast or five times that of Derry. Many Limerick workers faced low wages, lack of permanent jobs, emigration, ill health, poor housing and high rents.

The Limerick Trades and Labour Council was established in May 1905 – some time after similar Irish cities – to cater almost exclusively for skilled workers. Pressure to form a council had come from the Irish TUC who had complained that Limerick had failed to manage a respectable representation even once a year at the congress. Some time later, a Federated Labour Council was formed to look after the interests of unskilled workers.

The trades council was dominated by men whose sole concern seemed to be the protection of their craft status. They were pre-occupied with policies on maintaining apprenticeship rules, strict ratios of journeymen to apprentices and opposition to mechanisation or other innovations that might weaken their position in the market place.

Even before 1905 the trade unions had been active in local politics, but in a sporadic and uncoordinated way. They confined themselves largely to endorsing sympathetic candidates. These people generally supported the unions on issues like the direct employment by Limerick Corporation of its own building workers or an insistence on the use of trade union labour in public contracts given to private employers.

Many members of the trades council were fairly suspicious of the new politics emanating from "advanced" trade union elements in Dublin, particularly after the Irish TUC decision of 1912 to form an Irish Labour Party. In 1916 John Cronin, who later led the soviet, was prepared to characterise the Dublin leadership as a "socialist clique" and feared that "the movement was run entirely by people who never worked at any trade or labour or were at present not

THE DOCKS LIMERICK. 2677. W.L.

*Limerick docks in the early part of this century. The unloading of
seven thousand tons of bread-making grain was a
major boost to the soviet.*

following any trade or labour". [2] Nevertheless, some trade union activists in Limerick had been influenced by the events of the 1913 Lock Out in Dublin, by Connolly's writings and by his part in the 1916 rising. [3] James Larkin, speaking at the 1914 Irish Trade Union Congress paid a special tribute to the Limerick pork butchers who had "sent more every week in proportion to their strength than any other union" in assisting the locked-out workers. [4]

The arrival of the ITGWU in Limerick, in October 1917 was the catalyst for the trades council's transformation. The council supported the new union, and urged unskilled workers to join its ranks. The ITGWU responded by affiliating to the council rather than to the unskilled workers' Federated Labour Council. The trades council rapidly changed from being a localised, relatively backward, craft-dominated body into a broadly based, well-organised movement that could later lead the city in a time of crisis and dare to challenge the government.

In May 1918, the ITGWU national executive sent Joseph O'Connor to organise membership in the city. The first breakthrough was the incorporation within a month of Cleeves' workforce into the union. By the end of 1918 the ITGWU claimed to have over 3,000 Limerick city members and a wave of farm labourers' strikes had built up the membership in the county.

Another event in October 1917 considerably sharpened the workers' trade union and political responses. This was the appearance of Limerick's first working-class newspaper, *The Bottom Dog*. On 20 October the first issue outlined the *Dog*'s aim: "He believes in the truth of the old saying that 'Every dog has his day', but at the same time he must assert that the Bottom Dog's day appears to be a long way off, shrouded in the misty future. The work at hand then hastening the day of the Bottom Dog." [5] The paper defined the "Bottom Dog" as the oppressed – whether by nation, class or sex.

The paper strongly backed the Transport Union, saying that before its arrival the ordinary labourer had been "down in the dust simply for the want of unity and organisation". [6] It insisted the Bottom Dog would only come into his own when every worker, male and female, was thoroughly organised.

For the first time, the *Bottom Dog* brought together the forces of industrial unionism and the radical element among the craft unions. It was written and circulated by prominent members of Limerick United Trades and Labour Council and it could call on the services of sympathetic compositors and typographers. Ben Dineen, a baker, was the paper's editor. In November 1918, thirty-nine-year-old Dineen, together with two of his young children, succumbed to the ravages of the European-wide influenza. Up to his death, forty-eight editions of the paper had been published, though there is evidence that the *Dog* may have limped on for one or two more editions after the editor's death. The editorial policy of the *Bottom Dog* was a curious mixture. It had an extraordinarily hazy concept of socialism, based more on practical and pragmatic opposition to bad social conditions than on any thought out theoretical position. The paper veered frequently from advocating a syndicalist policy of taking power through industrial action to advocating the need for a socialist political party. Mixed in with this, was a strong ration of nationalism, some Catholic piety, a bigoted sectarian attitude towards Protestants, some anti-Semitism and an emphasis on local Limerick issues to the virtual exclusion of earthshaking events like World War I or the Bolshevik Revolution.

It would be wrong to overemphasise the *Bottom Dog's* influence on events in Limerick. Yet its witty tabloid-style of journalism made it popular and widely read, even in the rural areas of the county, as the ITGWU spread its membership during 1918. Given the paper's editorial content, it could not be said to have helped develop a socialist consciousness among Limerick workers. Yet, the constant and uncompromising references to bad housing, low pay and poor working conditions must have heightened some form of radical consciousness in the city. The new militancy in Limerick was manifested during 1918 in a large number of long strikes. The year started with unrest on the docks over pay and mechanisation. A plumbers' strike lasted almost four months until April and there was a three month long bakers' strike.

However, co-operation in the production of the *Bottom Dog* was not enough to prevent the clashes with the craft unions over "who represents whom" that were a hallmark of the growth of the ITGWU elsewhere. In May 1918 the delegate board of the Mechanics' Institute tried to reduce the influence of the ITGWU and the *Bottom Dog* by starting a second paper, *The Worker*. [7] It lacked the political and industrial bite of the *Dog* and concentrated instead on faithful reporting of the trades council and its affiliates. The move could be interpreted as an attempt to reduce the influence of the *Bottom Dog* and the ITGWU.

Limerick workers celebrated Labour Day for the first time ever in 1918. [8] On Sunday, 5 May an estimated 10,000 to 15,000 workers marched through the city streets in response to a call from the trades council. The demonstration ended with speeches from eighteen speakers standing on three platforms at the Markets' Field, where to the sound of a trumpet the assembled workers passed a resolution.

The first part of the resolution showed where some Limerick workers were deriving their inspiration. It read: "That we the workers of Limerick assembled, extend fraternal greetings to the workers of all countries, paying particular attention to our Russian comrades who have waged such a magnificent struggle for their social and political emancipation."[9] Michael Keyes, of the Railwaymens' Union, seconding the resolution, said Limerick had the reputation of being one of the best organised Labour centres in the country. The baker, Ben Dineen, secretary of the trades council, said the national strike against conscription, less than a fortnight previously, had shown that "Labour was supreme to all parties"[10] Limerick, he said, had been the first city in Ireland to put forth the propaganda

*Limerick military barracks in the early years of this century,
with a Scottish regiment on parade.*

of downing tools against conscription, a boast that was greeted with cheers. Robert O'Connor said he supposed they would be called Bolsheviks because they extended greetings to the Russian workers, but Irishmen could claim that as a small nation they had put backbone into any part of the world they were in. Again, this comment was met with cheers.

The influence and standing of the trades council may also be judged from the fact that its meetings were regularly and extensively reported in the local papers. A clue as to how the council stood on the broad issue of syndicalism may be gleaned from the minutes of a council discussion on the revised draft constitution of the combined Irish Labour Party and Trade Union Congress, which had been circulated to affiliated bodies.

The draft 1918 constitution renamed the movement to emphasise the fact that both the political and trade union elements were united in the one movement, a classical syndicalist position. It aimed to recover the nation's wealth and to win for workers, collectively, the ownership and control of the whole produce of their labour. Industry and services would be democratically managed and controlled by the whole body of workers involved, both manual and mental. In its aims and methods, it listed industrial and social organisation ahead of political. The Limerick council agreed to the name and objectives as set out, and quibbled only about details of how individual membership and trade union corporate membership of the congress party could be reconciled.

The stirrings of nationalism also found a response in Limerick. In 1917 and 1918 two new papers published in the city reflected this. These were *The Factionist* and *The Soldier Hunter.* [11] The first issue of the *Soldier Hunter* in February 1918 made it clear it would be a weekly watchdog against the moral corruption of the young women of Limerick by the British garrison. "We are out to clean up the town. Social Hygiene, if you will, is our objective," the paper thundered. [12] The paper listed many streets on the outskirts of Limerick that, it claimed, were "dens of infamy where immorality stalks naked and unabashed".

The *Soldier Hunter* realised the clergy had been doing "police work as well as priest's work" and this would have to be supplemented by tougher tactics. [13] The paper carried a plaintive letter from Father Dwane, administrator of St. Michael's parish, complaining about a military chaplain who had been assaulted by a Welsh fusilier when he had sought "to protect a girl of sixteen years of age against the lustful passion of this low clodhopper". [14] Another report told of a "khaki-clad demon" who had tried to seduce a young girl by "offering her drugged chocolates". [15] Small, local papers of this kind became a powerful weapon in the propaganda war between Sinn Féin and the government. Early in 1917, the intelligence officer for the southern military district had commented: "A determined effort is being made to spread extremist ideas by means of so-called newspapers, containing no current news, which circulate largely throughout the district... Papers of this kind... do an immense amount of harm among the semi-educated people who are their readers, and who notice the Government do not interfere with them or contradict their mis-statements."[16]

But the real turning point in the development of separatist politics locally was the release of the 1916 rising internees and the lifting of martial law on 21 January 1917. Those decisions released to Limerick, as to other parts of the country, men who had become hardened rather than embittered and who were determined to organise for a final push to freedom.

Within a month, the first Sinn Féin clubs were formed in the county. In June an estimated 7,000 people turned out to hear Michael Collins, the military and intelligence genius of the coming revolution, address a public meeting. In November, 12,000 people welcomed home the Republican hunger strikers, many more than had received the released internees almost a year before.

Membership of Sinn Féin and the Volunteers in Limerick increased in line with these changing circumstances. At the end of June 1917 Sinn Féin had 1,661 members and the Volunteers had 943. In May of 1918 the numbers were 4,000 and 1,912 respectively and by January 1919 there were over 4,600 Sinn Féin members and over 2,600 Volunteers.

Early in 1918 Sinn Féin and the trades council became allies in an agitation to prevent the live export of pigs to Britain because of the resultant loss of processing jobs in the city. With a capacity to kill up to 15,000 pigs a week, the city's factories were getting only 2,000. British buyers, with good contracts to fill, were prepared to pay well over the official recommended price and live exports of pigs were booming.

The conscription crisis of April 1918 saw Limerick trades council play the same leading role locally as the Irish TUC was doing nationally. After the government's intentions were announced, Limerick was the only trades council to actually call for a general strike. The call came the day after the trades council had led a demonstration of about 10,000 people, including Sinn Féiners and Irish Party members, against conscription. Even the banks were closed and the *Bottom Dog* claimed only two shops and two workers defied the strike call. [17]

In the 1918 mayoral election, the Sinn Féin supporter Alphonsus O'Mara was elected, replacing a Unionist sympathiser, Sir Stephen Quinn. Shortly after his election, the Limerick branch of the Irish Post Office Clerks' Association held a public meeting to protest against the dismissal from his job of their chairman, Robert Byrne, and the new mayor shared a platform with the trades council to denounce what he called "star chamber" methods.

The new year of 1919 saw a strengthening of opposition to the government and further support for separatism in Limerick. In his confidential monthly report to Dublin Castle for January, County Inspector Yates of the RIC reported that the outward state of the city and county was peaceable but under the surface it was unsettled and uncertain. There was a strong undercurrent of discontent and disloyalty and the outlook for the future was not good.

The influence of the ITGWU was spreading, according to Yates. The following month, after several strikes organised by the ITGWU, he was of the opinion that the union was rather overshadowing the active local Sinn Féin clubs. On St. Patrick's Day 1919, in Adare Co. Limerick, the closeness of the two seditious forces was underlined by a joint meeting of Sinn Féin and the ITGWU, addressed by a Catholic curate and a union organiser. While the police reported a static membership for the Volunteers and a small increase in Sinn Féin numbers, the number of ITGWU branches increased from fifteen to twenty-three, and membership in the city and county totalled over 3,800.

These confluent trends of trade unionism and nationalism were almost personified in the life and personality of Robert Byrne. Byrne was prominent in nationalist politics as adjutant of the Second Limerick Brigade, IRA. He was also president of the Limerick branch of the Post Office Clerks' Association and he represented them on the Limerick United Trades and Labour Council.

His imprisonment on arms charges, and his hunger strike and death in a mêlée with the RIC were the sparks that lit Limerick's fuse.

CHAPTER FOUR

Robert Byrne, Republican Trade Unionist

"Mr R. Byrne of Limerick Post Office, when viewing the decorations in
St. Ita's Hall, is alleged to have said that the flags would have to come
down as no one would dance under the Union Jack … "
*Police report on alleged disloyalty of postal officials in
the City of Limerick, January 1917*

Robert Byrne was shot in his bed in Limerick Workhouse Hospital on the
afternoon of Sunday, 6 April 1919 in a struggle with members of the Royal Irish
Constabulary. [1] The shooting took place during an attempted rescue of Byrne by
members of the IRA and, within a few hours, he had bled to death from his
wounds.

Twenty-eight-year-old Robert Byrne lived with his mother and father at Town
Wall Cottage in Limerick. Byrne was a cousin of the famous lord mayor of
Dublin and former National Party MP, Alfie Byrne, and his father was a Dublin
man from the North Strand. His mother was from Limerick.

Town Wall was an old historic part of Limerick nestling below the walls that
had witnessed the Williamite sieges of 1690 and 1691. It was reputed to be the
place where the women of Limerick had marshalled to repel the Orange besiegers. The area had a strong nationalist tradition which influenced Byrne's
outlook and for a number of years he had been active in the Sinn Féin movement.

Robert Byrne was employed as a telegraphist in the General Post Office in
Limerick. As far back as 1916, his name had been included in a list of post office
officials who had "come under the notice of the Police by reason of their
connection with the Irish Volunteer or Sinn Féin movements". The list shows
an entry as follows: "Byrne, Clerk, Limerick, Reported to be Sinn Féiner – No
action taken". [2]

In January 1917 Byrne came under closer scrutiny from the Police Crime
Branch (Special) in an investigation of "alleged disloyalty of Postal officials" in
Limerick. [3] Sinn Féin in Limerick often hired St. Ita's hall for Sunday night

dances. The drapers' assistants employed by Todds, the leading general store, had arranged to hold a dance in the same hall on a Wednesday night and had decorated the hall in preparation. Among the decorations used were the flags of the war time Allies, including the Union Jack.

Limerick postal officials had booked the same hall for a dance on the Saturday prior to the Sinn Féin event. On the morning of the postal dance, "Mr R. Byrne of the Limerick Post Office" when viewing the decorations, was alleged to have said the flags would have to come down as no one would dance under the Union Jack.

On another occasion during that day, a police report noted that Byrne had said the postal officials were afraid to leave up the flags for fear the Sinn Féiners would interfere with them at their regular Sunday night dance.

Because of the postal clerks' objections, the drapers' assistants took down all the decorations. But the episode meant only a handful of postal officials attended their Saturday night dance, perhaps fearing that association with the event might damage their careers.

Robert Byrne's star continued to rise in the Republican firmament. Just before Christmas 1918, he was elected adjutant of the Second Battalion, Limerick Brigade, of the IRA. But the tolerance of the authorities had reached its limits. In January 1919 Byrne was dismissed from the post office for attending the funeral of a Limerick Volunteer named John Daly.[4] In a report headed "The Hidden Hand in the GPO", the *Bottom Dog* grimly noted the "esteemed and respected" Byrne's dismissal. It warned that he would have the support of the Post Office Clerks' Association and the trade union movement generally. [5]

Within days of losing his job his mother's house was raided for arms. On 13 January 1919 Byrne was arrested by the RIC and charged with possession of a revolver and ammunition. According to some accounts, Byrne's colleagues believed these items had been planted on him.

Byrne was court-martialled and sentenced to twelve months' imprisonment with hard labour for being in possession of a revolver and ammunition. The official court-martial records show such a sentence passed on "Robert T. Byrnes" of Limerick on either 2 or 4 February – one date has been typed on top of the other and it is therefore difficult to say which is the intended date. [6]

Byrne quickly asserted himself as leader of the Republican prisoners in Limerick Jail but he found himself in a prison system where solitary confinement and cruelty were the order of the day, and the prisoners' response was the terrible double-edged sword of the hunger strike.

Early in January, the *Irish Independent* had reported a meeting held at the O'Connell Monument in Limerick to protest at the treatment of political prisoners in the local prison. [7] The Catholic bishop of Limerick, Dr Denis Hallinan, described the prisoners' treatment as "a gross breach of the promise made by the

Government in Ireland on the death of Thomas Ashe". [8] Ashe died on 25 September 1917 as a result of force feeding in Mountjoy Prison, in Dublin, during a hunger strike. The Limerick meeting was reported to be "of large dimensions, although called at an hour's notice". [9] Significantly, in view of later events, the speakers included John Cronin, president of Limerick United Trades and Labour Council.

Then, as in later years, the demand of Republican prisoners was to be treated as political prisoners, not subject to the ordinary prison routine, and under their own military discipline.

Finding that peaceful methods were of no avail in advancing their demands, the Republican prisoners resorted to other methods. Within days of his imprisonment, as senior officer, Robert Byrne started a campaign of disobedience. The prison authorities sent for RIC reinforcements. The prisoners were beaten, their boots and clothing removed. They were handcuffed, some were kept in solitary confinement and given only bread and water.

Led by Byrne, the prisoners rioted, wrecking cells and smashing fittings. Again, they were overpowered by the sheer force of RIC reinforcements. The official press censor prevented the *Irish Independent* from reporting the disturbance. [10] Byrne resorted to the final weapon – a hunger strike.

The official prison board records for this period were removed from Dublin Castle when the British administration finally withdrew in 1922, so it is difficult to put an exact date on the commencement of Byrne's hunger strike. However, contemporary newspaper reports suggest it was in the third week of February.

The events in Limerick Prison were reported to the office of the chief secretary for Ireland on a daily basis. The files there recorded the commencement of Byrne's hunger strike [11] and a discussion of the granting of what was termed "amelioration" to him. There was a general report on the "disorderly conduct" of prisoners and a report on damage to prison property by Robert J. Byrne and James Kennedy. One interesting document was entitled "Limerick: Damage to prison property and list of mutinous DORA prisoners" (DORA prisoners were those arrested and imprisoned under the Defence of the Realm Act). The Castle records note that this file was transferred to the Irish Free State Department of Justice on 5 May 1925, when that fledgeling state presumably faced similar problems in its prisons.

Although the authorities did not attempt to force feed Robert Byrne, force feeding of prisoners was a major issue in Limerick during February 1919. On 8 February, A.F. Falkiner, governor of Limerick Prison, sent Max Green, the chairman of the General Prisons Board, a copy of what he termed a "placard" posted in Limerick that evening. [12] The leaflet referred to "the horrible and revolting system of forcible feeding" and accused two Limerick doctors of "doing [their] dirty work!".

The doctors were named as McGrath and Irwin. Dr P.J. Irwin was stated, in the leaflet, to be resident medical officer at the Limerick District Asylum "at a salary of close on £1,000 per annum". [13] The leaflet alleged Irwin was ready to put the life of a fellow-countryman in danger for the sake of an additional three guineas a week. Also on the night of February 8, a dozen similar leaflets were found in the letter box at Limerick post office.

On 13 February, District Inspector Craig of the RIC submitted a report on the leafletting incidents to the force's inspector general. [14] Both doctors were stated to be popular and not in any danger. Dr M.S. McGrath FRCS had one of the city dispensaries, and was medical officer of health as well as being prison medical officer. During 1917 and 1918, the doctor did a good deal to highlight Limerick's appalling slum housing in a series of three articles he wrote for the *Bottom Dog*. Inspector Craig noted that McGrath's private practice was not large, and that for the present he was not likely to suffer professional injury. "But," the district inspector remarked, "if he has to forcibly feed sinn féin [sic] prisoners in the future it is very probable that he will become unpopular." [15]

On the same day, Limerick Asylum Board met to consider the actions of Dr Irwin, their resident medical officer. [16] Dr Irwin denied he had left the asylum to force feed prisoners for an additional three guineas a week. He claimed he had been acting on foot of the general rules for the management of the asylum and in accordance with the practice of his predecessor over fifteen years.

The Asylum Board adopted a resolution expressing considerable indignation at Irwin's action, and noting that he had promised he would refuse to continue assisting in force feeding.

Dr Irwin's withdrawal was reported to the General Prisons Board on 14 February by Dr McGrath in his capacity as medical officer of Limerick Prison.[17] Dr McGrath requested that arrangements be made to get a consultant from somewhere else, with recognised experience, to assist in any further recourse to force feeding. His view was that there were no members of the medical profession in Limerick on whom he could count to consult with him if the question arose again.

Dublin Castle studied the general rules and regulations for the management of the Limerick District Asylum, drawn up in 1912, to see if the asylum resident medical superintendent could be forced to assist the prison doctor. [18] Rule five stated: "The Resident Medical Superintendent shall superintend and regulate the whole establishment ... He shall devote the whole of his time to his office ... He shall, however, be permitted to undertake the following engagements – visiting any person at the request of the Lord Lieutenant, the Lord Chancellor, the General Prisons Board, the Inspectors of Lunatics, or one of them, examining into such person's mental state, reporting, and, if necessary, giving evidence thereon." The Castle concluded, correctly, that there was nothing in this rule to authorise Dr Irwin's assistance at force feeding in the prison.

Since Dr Irwin's withdrawal almost coincided with the start of Robert Byrne's hunger strike, that may explain why the prison authorities did not try to force feed Byrne. The strain of force feeding, and its unpopularity, obviously took its toll on Dr McGrath. In 1919, he applied for a salary increase and later in the same year he resigned as medical officer of Limerick Prison. [19]

The treatment of the prisoners did not go without local protest. The mayor and corporation discussed the situation and wrote to the Castle authorities protesting at the sentences and treatment of Byrne and a prisoner named Moran. Once again the press censor deleted the major portion of the *Independent's* report. [20] This told how the prisoners were handcuffed and lashed with ropes in their cells, deprived of their food, papers and tobacco and how the police had assaulted the prisoners. A public meeting was also held to protest against the treatment of the prisoners. Understandably, since Robert Byrne was a delegate representing the post office clerks, Limerick Trades Council joined in the protests. At a meeting on February 14 – when pressure on the two doctors was at its height – the council adopted a resolution and later distributed it throughout the city in leaflet form under the heading "The Jail Infamy in Limerick". [21] This leaflet was duly noted in the files of Dublin Castle as a "Sinn Féin" leaflet. The trades council resolution read: "That we the members of Limerick Trades and Labour Council, assembled in conference, protest most emphatically against the treatment meted out to the political prisoners at present confined in Limerick County Jail, and view with grave alarm the inactivity of the Visiting Justices and Medical Officer. Furthermore, we call on the public representatives to do their duty to their fellow-countrymen and take the necessary steps to have the prisoners receive what they are justly entitled to, namely political treatment; that copies of this resolution be submitted to the local Press, Visiting Justices and Medical Officer."

The trades council leaflet contrasted the treatment of the Republican prisoners with that of a man convicted of the manslaughter of a girl "in circumstances of the most revolting brutality". He had been sentenced by a judge "lenient to his ilk" to serve twelve months in the first division of the prison. The killer was not required to work, according to the leaflet, and he was supplied with every comfort – a cot, books, newspapers, slippers, glass, writing materials. "In fact," the leaflet claimed, he had "everything he could procure in a first-class hotel."

In an emotional appeal, the council suggested that men "who have never committed a crime" believed they were entitled at least to the treatment the criminal was getting. It said that one of the prisoners – Henry Meany – was in a bad state of health, yet was manacled as well as handcuffed. Meany was subsequently removed to Mountjoy Prison in Dublin in a very critical condition.

Hunger strikes, force feeding and protests were not confined to Limerick. By

April 1919, prisoners in Dublin, Belfast and Cork had spent as many as fourteen weeks in solitary confinement in disputes over their treatment as political prisoners. After three weeks of his hunger strike, the prison authorities became worried about Byrne's condition. Between 6 March and 8 March Byrne became confined to bed in the prison hospital. On 12 March, he was removed to no. 1 ward of Limerick Workhouse, or the Union Infirmary as it was also called. This ward was on the second floor, near the infirmary gates.

The Limerick IRA sensed an opportunity to boost morale and embarrass the authorities by rescuing Byrne from the less secure confines of the workhouse. Commandant Peadar Dunne called a battalion council meeting in Hogan's, next door to Matt Boland's shop in Gerald Griffin Street. A plan was agreed, to be executed on Sunday, 6 April. [22]

Twenty-four IRA men were to enter the ward under the guise of visitors and a covering party of fifteen would be on duty in the corridors and grounds. According to one account, only Michael "Batty" Stack, section leader of E Company, would be armed, though a not necessarily fully reliable contemporary report suggests two members of the rescue party were armed. On the day, there was a hitch in the transport arrangements. The battalion driver had to leave Limerick city urgently to help Dan Breen and Sean Hogan – still wanted for their part in the January killing of RIC members at Soloheadbeg – escape through a British military cordon. Instead, a mourning coach was procured from a local undertaker, with a nurse inside ready with clothes and a disguise for Byrne.

The RIC had general orders to shoot prisoners in circumstances where a rescue was being attempted. That Sunday afternoon, Robert Byrne was being closely guarded by Sergeant J.F. Goulden or Golden of Ballyneety, Co. Limerick, Constable J. Tierney of Kilteely, Constable J. Fitzpatrick of Clarina, Constable Martin O'Brien who was attached to Caherconlish Station, Constable T. Spillane of Askeaton Station and Warder John Mahoney or Mahony, Rocksborough Road, who was on the staff of Limerick Jail. [23]

As the hands of the clock moved toward to three, the pitch of conversation rose as visitors tried to cram into the remaining minutes the things that had been left unsaid. IRA-man Paddy Dawson checked his watch, and blew a shrill whistle in a pre-arranged signal.

All the accounts of what happened next agree it was a short decisive affray. According to the warder, two men presented revolvers and ordered "Hands Up!". Several revolver shots rang out and patients jumped beneath their beds in terror as panic-stricken visitors scattered. People out for a Sunday afternoon stroll turned back in fright at the sound of gunfire. Constable Martin O'Brien was already firing.

As soon as the whistle was blown, Warder Mahony, Constable Spillane and another policeman ran to the bed and grabbed Byrne as he tried to rise. Constable

Spillane had his revolver out, and as Robert Byrne tried to heave himself out of bed, the burly policeman hurled himself bodily on top of him. Sometime during this confused struggle, a bullet entered the body of Robert Byrne, on the left-hand side, between the sixth and seventh ribs. From a range of four feet, Batty Stack shattered Spillane's spine with a bullet from a .38 revolver. A second shot from Stack, and eighteen-stone Constable O'Brien collapsed to the floor in an ungainly heap.

Clad only in his nightshirt and an overcoat, Byrne staggered down the stairs, supported by two comrades. By mistake, the coach driver had gone round to the mortuary at the back of the hospital. Byrne and his companions were forced on to the public road. They had gone only 300 yards, towards Hassett's Cross, when they stopped a pony and trap driven by John Ryan of Knockalisheen, Co. Clare, and his daughter Nancy. They brought the wounded IRA man to their labourer's cottage, near Meelick in Co. Clare. There, at half past eight on Sunday, 6 April, Robert Byrne died.[24]

Earlier, in the workhouse, Constable Martin O'Brien had died too. At his request, a clergyman was sent for and the chaplain, Canon O'Driscoll, administered the last rites to the dying man. Constable Spillane's wound, close to his spine, was also serious but the other policemen and the warder sustained only minor injuries, probably caused by blows from a truncheon that was later found in the ward. There were bullet marks on the walls and a statue of the Infant of Prague on a little altar had been damaged by a ricochet.

Constable O'Brien was a married man, with one child. One report gives his age as fifty, but another states he was thirty-five, with twelve years' service in the constabulary. O'Brien was stationed in Caherconlish, in Co. Limerick, and he had been on temporary duty in the city for only three weeks. He was buried in his native Birr, Co. Offaly. There was a large attendance at the funeral, including senior Catholic clergy, and there were fifty cars in the cortège. In a sign that bitterness had not yet run too deep, some members of Sinn Féin attended the funeral.

The lord lieutenant, Lord French, sent his condolences to Mrs O'Brien, as did the inspector-general of the RIC. Mrs O'Brien demanded £2,000 in compensation for the death of her husband. Dublin Castle records later show a grant made to the constable's mother, [25] an application by his widow to be made post mistress of Caherconlish in Co. Limerick, and the grant to her of a pension of two pounds a week. Constable Spillane, son of an RIC sergeant from Loughrea in Co. Galway, was also awarded a pension. He was lucky to have survived – he was removed to Dublin for treatment where surgeons discovered and removed the bullet lodged in his spine.

The area around the house in Meelick, where Robert Byrne died, was placed under military control and there was much police and military activity in

Counties Clare and Limerick. One of the few documents of the time still extant in Dublin Castle is a telegram from County Inspector Yates, of the RIC, reporting the finding of Byrne's body. [26] The telegram was dispatched at 1.53 pm and received in the chief secretary's office at 3.17 pm, on Monday, 7 April. It said the body had just been discovered at the house of John Ryan of Knockalisheen, Ardnacrusha sub-district, Co. Clare. Death had apparently been caused by a bullet wound in the stomach.

According to the telegram, the owner of the house, John Ryan, was arrested along with others found there: Arthur Johnson, Parnell Street, Limerick, John Hurley of Town Wall Cottage (a cousin of the deceased), the prisoner's mother, Mrs Byrne, Thomas Crowe of Sarsfield Street and Patrick Brady of Lower Gerald Griffin Street. Brady, it later emerged, had been sent from an undertaker's to measure the deceased for his coffin. Arthur Johnson had been Byrne's predecessor as adjutant and was now battalion engineer in the IRA; Hurley later became quarter master of the mid-Limerick brigade of the IRA.

Robert Byrne had the attentions of one, and possibly two doctors and a priest before he died. His body lay on a bed in an upper storey of Ryan's house and on his naked breast, close to the heart, was a hole the size of a halfpenny. The bullet had passed through his lungs, causing a fatal haemorrhage. Near the bed was a bloodstained Volunteer's overcoat. Mrs Ryan said that the men who had brought Byrne to the house were complete strangers to her, but they had asked her, in the name of God, to take him in.

The authorities kept a close watch on the Meelick cottage. It was surrounded by detachments of police and the Scottish horse regiment. On her way there, the vehicle in which Mrs Byrne travelled had been preceded and followed by military lorries. She was promptly arrested when she arrived, along with four other women and John Ryan's wife, servant boy and servant girl. In the succeeding weeks, those who had been arrested were released.

The general meeting of Limerick trades council held on the Friday after Byrne's death dealt only with some matters of special importance. As a mark of respect to their late fellow-member, the president John Cronin suggested that they adjourn after the minutes had been read. [27] He said it was his sad duty to propose this resolution: "That a vote of condolence be sent to Mrs Byrne on the death of her son, who for the cause of self-determination as all Irishmen are entitled to, was murdered by the minions of English Tyranny here in our midst." [28] But while sympathising with Mrs Byrne's grief, Cronin said he must also congratulate her in having reared a son of such heroic disposition, whose name would be handed down in generations to come as an example of what an Irishman should be.

Mrs Byrne's letter in reply is preserved in the minute book of the council: "... Thank God that our dear son and brother died a free man fighting for his country's cause. I pray the Almighty that his blood has not been shed in vain and that our dear Motherland will soon shake off the shackles of the Foreigner and take her righteous place among the Nations of the Earth .... " [29] The letter's style is reminiscent of similar letters written, for example, by the executed leaders of the 1916 rising and their families. In later years, however, local people believed Mrs Byrne missed her son deeply and regretted his death to the point of bitterness.

Mrs Byrne's treatment at Meelick and the arrest of some of the prisoner's cousins led to protests later at a meeting of the Limerick Infirmary Guardians. There were incidents around William Street police station and reports of a baton charge in the city. Thus the first week of April 1919 ended amid stirring events and aroused passions.

However there was more to come, as people learned the details of Byrne's shooting and death and Limerick prepared to mourn a dead hero. The fuse had been lit and the flame had begun its inexorable journey to the powder keg.

CHAPTER FIVE

Funeral and Inquest

"The Government have no wish to interfere with the
solemnity and dignity of any funeral ceremonial, but they cannot tolerate
any defiance of the law."
Official communiqué issued on Wednesday, 9 April 1919,
in advance of Robert Byrne's funeral.

On Tuesday, 8 April, at Meelick, the coroner for East Clare, Michael Brady, opened an inquest into the death of Robert Byrne. The inquest began at John Ryan's cottage, where Byrne had died. The remains were identified by Sergeant James Walshe, a plain clothes member of the RIC from Limerick and by the deceased's brother, Thomas.

Dr T. Humphreys, resident medical officer to the workhouse and Dr James Brennan, visiting physician there, carried out the post-mortem examination. Dr Humphreys said there was a small circular external wound just below the heart, but he could not find a corresponding exit wound. He could not find the bullet, which had taken a backward and downward course. It penetrated the left lung and the walls of the stomach and apparently lodged in the intestines. In a portent of allegations yet to come, District Inspector McClelland of the RIC objected to a line of questioning and to the admission of evidence that suggested the fatal shot had been been fired at close range.

The doctors cited haemorrhage, peritonitis (inflammation of the intestines) and shock as the causes of death.

The coroner agreed to hand over Byrne's remains to his relatives for burial and adjourned the inquest for a week. Michael Brennan of Meelick, a leading member of the IRA, complained that the Volunteer uniform had been removed from Byrne and a file was indeed opened in Dublin Castle under the title "Robert Byrne – Forfeiture of Volunteer uniform". [1] This suggests the removal complained of was a deliberate act of policy.

An estimated 10,000 people attended the removal of Robert Byrne's body from John Ryan's house in Meelick to St. John's Cathedral in Limerick. The coffin, covered in the Republican tricolour, was borne three miles or so on the shoulders of Volunteers. Close on 10,000 mourners from Limerick and Clare marched in a military-style escort with the hearse.

During the parade, there was no police interference, as police and military had been withdrawn from the streets. But the authorities were not prepared to accept further open defiance. On the night of the removal, an assistant inspector general of the RIC visited Limerick, while Major Maunsell, chief intelligence officer, southern district, arrived with other military officers. Their visit was said to be in connection with the mapping out of a portion of Limerick to be placed under martial law. The following day, Wednesday, 9 April, the authorities' determination was underlined in an official communiqué issued as a public notice: "The Government have no wish to interfere with the solemnity and dignity of any funeral ceremonial, but they cannot tolerate any defiance of law. Anything in the shape of a military parade or assembly in military formation will at once be stopped. The Government will accept no responsibility for any consequences which may arise from disobedience of this order." [2]

All that day thousands of people passed by Robert Byrne's coffin, lying in state before the high altar in Limerick cathedral and the flag of the Town Hall flew at half mast.

On Thursday, 10 April, Robert Byrne was buried in Mount St. Laurence's Cemetery in Limerick. The funeral was as much a city's display of defiance as an expression of sorrow. There was a strong military presence throughout the day. Armoured cars flashed through the streets, and coming up to two o'clock, sections of soldiers with fixed bayonets and police took up positions along the funeral route. Each section was supported by an armoured car and an ambulance. A military aeroplane circled above the cathedral and followed the procession for part of the way.

At ten past three, the funeral left the cathedral. The hearse was covered in wreaths, and many more were carried by Volunteers following behind. The *Irish Independent* termed it "a most remarkable funeral demonstration. First came the Catholic clergy of the city churches, the wreath-bedecked hearse, the flag-draped coffin borne by Volunteers, the chief mourners and a seemingly endless number of Volunteers from Limerick, Clare and Tipperary with Cumann na mBan. A further 5,000 must have marched – including the mayor and members of the Corporation in state." [3]

The funeral made its way through the old town, the Mall, Patrick Street, William Street, to the cemetery. The mourning throngs wore armlets of crepe and the Sinn Féin colours of green, white and orange. As the coffin passed points where the military and police were posted, the troops presented arms. At the corner of O'Connell Street and William Street, the clatter of rifle butts on the cobbled setts and the glint of bayonets in the sunlight caused a moment of panic among the crowd. A few onlookers were slightly injured in a wild stampede.

Among the mourners at the graveside was the deceased's cousin Alfie Byrne, a former National Party MP, alderman of Dublin Corporation, and famous lord mayor of that city. The mourners also included railway workers and employees of some local stores who had taken the day off when refused a half holiday to attend the funeral. Already, the emotions aroused by Byrne's death were having their effects among some workers. Byrne's post office clerical colleagues in Limerick, Thurles and Limerick junction and the Limerick postmen laid wreaths at the grave. His brother, Thomas, worked as a chemist's assistant and the assistants' association passed a vote of condolence. More significant perhaps was the vote of sympathy passed by the ITGWU on the night of the burial.

With the funeral of Robert Byrne over, public attention could focus again on the precise and increasingly controversial circumstances of his death. The issues arose with devastating clarity, not in the resumed inquest on Byrne himself, but in the more unlikely forum of the inquest on Constable O'Brien.

The Byrne family retained Patrick Lynch KC to represent their interests at the O'Brien inquest and at Byrne's own inquest. Lynch was a member of a prominent nationalist family who had unsuccessfully challenged Eamon de Valera in the crucial East Clare by-election of July 1917. In the subsequent years of the War of Independence, he represented Republican interests in a number of celebrated trials and inquests.

Lynch first questioned the legality of Byrne's detention at the workhouse hospital during the adjourned inquest on Byrne himself. But, the following day, in the inquest on Constable O'Brien, he developed the idea and made a sustained legal attack on the validity of the detention. By undermining the legality of Byrne's detention, Lynch's aim was to dissuade the jury from bringing in a "verdict at large" – in simple terms, implicating a person or persons unknown in the killing of the policeman.

Lynch began his final speech to the jury by emphasising the wide powers of a coroner's court. [4] It could issue a warrant for the arrest of anybody, who could then be tried without any intermediate intervention by a magistrate. If the jury returned a verdict beyond the actual cause of death, they would be opening up a very large field of investigation, he said.

The inquiry, according to Lynch, had been conducted in a very singular way. They had evidence that Byrne was a patient in the hospital, but none to show he was sentenced to imprisonment or that he was a prisoner on the day of the rescue, any more than any other patient in the hospital. If friends and relatives came to take away a patient, what right had anyone to stop them? Byrne was not a prisoner, he argued, and how did his case differ from that of any other patient?

Lynch said the jury could not bring in a verdict against people or attribute crimes to them without evidence, and the jury were not to assume that because a warder took up position beside him that Byrne was in legal custody. The police were bound to prevent a prisoner being taken from them, and they would be justified in using a great deal of force in doing so, but there was no pretence in this case that Byrne was their prisoner.

"If the matter was probed and investigated," said Lynch, "it would be found that men who were ill and transferred from other prisons to hospitals for treatment did not leave in the custody or company of a warder because there was no legal sanction to send one. If that were so, the warder John Mahony had no more right in the ward than anyone who might be a trespasser, except he was there with the courtesy of the Infirmary Guardians. He had no right to hold Byrne once he left the walls of Limerick Prison, and neither the warder nor the police had any right to detain him in the hospital. "

In legal terms, the inescapable conclusion to be drawn from Lynch's argument was that Byrne was not held in legal custody at the time of the shooting. Therefore, any violence used by the police or warders to restrain him had no legal backing. His death from a bullet wound sustained in the infirmary struggle could, therefore, be characterised as contrary to law – either murder or manslaughter.

In Dublin Castle, the authorities requested a legal opinion on the legality of police remaining in an infirmary to prevent the escape of a prisoner. [5] The Castle records indicate this request referred to a case in Cork infirmary. It may, indeed, have referred to Cork, though the relevant file number is contemporaneous with the events in Limerick. The file is no longer held in Dublin Castle, but the records note it was handed over to the Irish Free State department of justice on 5 May, 1925 – an interesting example of the similarity, and continuity perhaps, of the problems faced by the new state.

In any event, Lynch's eloquent plea had the desired effect locally. In Constable O'Brien's case, the jury perfunctorily returned a verdict that his death was due to haemorrhage, the result of a bullet wound. They did not, therefore, seem to take any account of a plea from the crown solicitor for Limerick, J.S. Gaffney, that the .38 calibre bullet found in the constable's body indicated he had been shot by a non-constabulary weapon.

The following day, at the conclusion of Robert Byrne's inquest, a different jury showed no hesitation. After only twenty minutes deliberation, they found that "Robert J. Byrne met his death by a revolver bullet discharged by either Constable O'Brien or Constable Spillane". [6] Here, the decisive evidence was that of Dr. John Holmes, of Barrington's Hospital, who spent the last hour or so with Byrne before he died.

Holmes asked the dying man, "How did this happen to you?" [7]

He replied, "I was jumping out of bed."

"Do you know who did it to you?" asked Holmes.

"The man that was shot," replied Byrne.

"That was all he said", continued the witness, "that was relevant as to how he sustained the wounds."

This evidence pointed towards either Constable O'Brien or Spillane (since both were "shot") as the man who had pulled the trigger on Robert Byrne. But first, there was legal argument as to whether Byrne's words could be admitted in evidence.

Dr Holmes said he saw Byrne at about seven o'clock on the evening he died, and he was vomiting blood about every quarter of an hour. Byrne said to him, "This is going to do for me doctor. Is it not?" Then he said, "I am not afraid to die, in any case."

The state solicitor, Gaffney, pointed out that there were only two cases where a dying declaration was admissible in evidence. One was where there was a charge of murder against a person then on trial, and the other was in the case of manslaughter and in the presence of the person being indicted for that manslaughter.

Lynch's reply was clever. Murder and manslaughter were both charges arising from the death of someone, but in an inquest too, it was a death they were dealing with. In such a case, he argued, what more powerful evidence could there be than the "voice from the grave" ? If the deceased man knew he was dying – if he knew he was in a dying condition – and if counsel could produce evidence for the coroner and the jury incriminating any person, then the jury could bring in a verdict against the person incriminated, and on their finding, the coroner could issue his warrant for the arrest of such person. If the jury had power to issue a warrant and bring in a verdict, they had the same power to receive evidence to justify a warrant. If the evidence led to a conviction afterwards, surely the hearing of such evidence in the first place was admissible?

P.J. Kelly, one of the resident magistrates for Limerick city, witnessed much of the inquest and sent a graphic account of the proceedings that day to the under secretary at Dublin Castle. [8] Kelly expressed concern about the inflammatory nature of comments made about him by O'Brien Moran, a solicitor representing Arthur Johnson, one of those arrested when Byrne's body was found. The solicitor general advised the under secretary that the coroner had discretion about how he conducted proceedings, unless they were irregular and could be quashed by the High Court. As regards speeches, nothing could be done, unless proceedings were justified against the speakers.

Kelly's report said that more than 500 people were present in Limerick city courthouse for Byrne's inquest. There were frequent bursts of loud applause, and cheering, according to Kelly. From the extended report on the inquest in the *Irish Independent* we get a flavour of Lynch's final speech to the jury. [9] From the evidence, said Lynch, they could gather that Byrne belonged to the Irish Volunteers, "a body recognised by everybody as remarkable for the purity of their lives, nobility of motives and their unselfish love of the land that bore them". That statement was received with prolonged cheering. Nearly sixty years later, in a series of conversations with the Limerick historian, Jim Kemmy, Batty Stack admitted it might have been a bullet from his gun that killed Robert Byrne. [10] The sixteen-year-old Stack himself did most of the shooting in the workhouse hospital ward. He fatally wounded Constable O'Brien, but may have unwittingly wounded the prisoner too, as a weakened Robert Byrne tried desperately to ease himself out of the line of fire. With the benefit of hindsight, then, the Crown solicitor's claim that the calibre of the bullet found in Constable O'Brien's body showed that he was killed by a non-constabulary weapon, is seen in a new light.

Within the IRA, Batty Stack had a reputation as a cool and efficient killer, a squat gunman who shot first and did not talk afterwards. Although IRA members often recounted their exploits in bolt holes like a favoured public house in Nelson Street, Stack was noted for his silence. In the aftermath of the workhouse rescue, his coolness stood to him and he allowed the British authorities to suffer the blame for the killing of Byrne, while he kept the truth to himself.

In the early months of 1919 Stack had taken part in numerous IRA operations. Although he lived in a largely Republican community, at Carey's Road near Limerick's railway station, Stack took little part in any overt anti-British demonstrations. Like others with military expertise, he was kept in the background for the "real" fight – the armed attacks on police and army.

Eventually, Stack's exploits came to the notice of Michael Collins, who was then intensifying the military campaign against British occupation. He was seconded to IRA headquarters, in Dublin, and became one of Collins' select and hand-picked assassins, whose activities had such a disproportionately devastating effect on the morale of the Crown forces. Stack would often disappear from Limerick for days on end and the few people "in the know" would scan the newspapers for details of the latest IRA shooting escapade.

The startling outcome of the inquests on O'Brien and Byrne was an unpleasant shock for the British authorities and the people of Limerick. But, while all of this was emerging behind the walls of the courthouse, other events had been taking place in Limerick and the shock of the inquests was as nothing compared to the tremors that were being prepared.

CHAPTER SIX

Soldiers and Strikers

"We, as organised workers refuse to ask them for permits to earn our daily
bread and this strike is a protest against their action."
John Cronin, chairman, Limerick strike committee

On Wednesday, 9 April 1919, Lieutenant-General the Right Honourable Sir
Frederick Shaw KCB, commander-in-chief Ireland, appointed Brigadier-
General C.J. Griffin as the competent military authority throughout Ireland. [1] In
a separate notice, most of Limerick city and a part of the county were placed
under General Griffin's authority, as a special military area. [2]

All of this was done under the provisions of the Defence of the Realm Acts
and the regulations made under the acts. This act – DORA as it was usually
known – was introduced by the British authorities early in World War I to give
them sweeping powers, literally, to defend the realm. One of its key provisions
was the power to proclaim entire districts as special military areas, under what
was termed a competent military authority. This enabled the military to issue
entrance and exit permits and to weed out spies by frequent and close checking
of passes. Later on, as the Anglo-Irish War increased in ferocity, special military
areas were used to pressurise the local citizenry into disowning the gunmen in
their midst.

General Shaw's signature simply gave legal effect to the authorities' swift
response, already announced, to the events in Limerick. On the Monday morning
after the shooting at the infirmary, the following official announcement was
issued: "In consequence of the attack by armed men on police constables and
the brutal murder of one of them at Limerick yesterday, the Government has
decided to proclaim the district as a special military area." [3]

As general officer in command of forces in Ireland, General Shaw attended
a top-level meeting that Monday morning at the Vice Regal Lodge in Dublin,
together with the heads of the Royal Irish Constabulary and the Dublin Metropolitan Police. Later the same day, the lord chancellor had a meeting with the
lord lieutenant, Viscount French.

Three days later, French and the chief secretary for Ireland, MacPherson, jointly sent an urgent, almost panic-stricken, demand for troop reinforcements to the adjutant-general in London: "The situation here grows worse and worse. It cannot be dealt with efficiently unless the eight battalions which were promised to the Chief Secretary by you are immediately sent. Five are understood to be ordered. These are not enough for the purpose. It is absolutely imperative that great expedition should be used in the dispatch of these troops."[4] In January, the war office had promised Dublin they would not be "let down" below the minimum requirements of troops and mechanical transport. Now the reply was that necessary steps were being taken to expedite the dispatch of troops.

Although the formal proclamation of the military area was made on Wednesday, 9 April, it was not to come into practical effect until the beginning of the following week. The military and police spent the intervening period mapping out the area to be covered, securing positions and selecting sites for military outposts leading to the city. They commandeered the extensive premises of the Shannon Rowing Club, something they had previously done after the disturbances of Easter week 1916.

Already, the *Irish Times* noted that respectable citizens "who took natural pride in the city's industries" were beginning to wonder how far they would be affected by the proclamation. [5] Most people, the newspaper said, realised the restrictions would seriously affect the commercial interests of the city. That was indeed a classic understatement. It was as if the regulations had been deliberately drafted to punish, if not provoke, the citizens of Limerick.

The Shannon was designated as the northern boundary of the special military area. Immediately, this meant the large working class area of Thomondgate, to the north, was cut off from the rest of the city. Workers from there would have to show permits and undergo military checks four times a day, on two bridges, as they went to and from their work. Similarly, workers who lived on the southern side of the river would face police and military scrutiny going to Thomondgate. Between 5,000 and 6,000 workers were directly affected by the restrictions. Two of the city's largest factories were north of the river and therefore cut off – Cleeves' Condensed Milk and Butter Company, employing 600 workers (mostly women) and Walkers' Distillery.

Entire suburbs had been divided under the regulations and the supply of milk to the city, mostly from Cleeves, would be seriously disrupted. Tenants who held vegetable allotments in the rural area north of the Shannon would be unable to tend them.

People who needed permits were required to report to the offices of the military commandant, General Griffin, at no.78, O'Connell Street – the former recruiting office. They were required to produce a letter of identification from the RIC sergeant in their district. If the police thought the applicant was a fit person to get a permit, one whose loyalty was beyond doubt, they would

Not Transferable

No. 14471

AREA OF *Limerick*

DEFENCE OF THE REALM

LOCAL PASS

Limerick SPECIAL MILITARY AREA.

(210). Wt. 864. 3. 50,000. 5/18. J. F. G. 5.

One of thousands of military passes issued under the Defence of the Realm Act to control the movement of Limerick's citizens in April 1919, after the British government had declared the city a special military area.

recommend him to the military authorities. In this way, known Republican sympathisers faced economic punishment for their views, if they could not exercise their trade or vocation. In addition, people suspected of crimes could be isolated and taken into custody.

After the police recommendation, the military recorded the applicants' height, weight, colour of hair and eyes and other details. These were kept on a card, duly stamped and dated. In some cases, applicants faced the trouble of having to apply every day. Only children under the age of sixteen were permitted to cross the bridges without a permit.

At this time, people in seven districts in Ireland faced such restrictions. To add insult to injury, the ratepayers could be levied with half the cost of sending extra police to the area. In Westport, Co. Mayo, for example, no potatoes or other farm produce or turf were allowed in and poor people were suffering particularly badly because of the lack of fuel. Even most of the mourners at a funeral were turned back a mile outside the town. Trade union organisation and tradition, the frequent overlapping of membership between the Labour and Republican movements and the heightened passions after the death and funeral of Robert Byrne all ensured Limerick's response would be sterner, and more effective, than that of other areas.

The IRA man who pulled the trigger at the workhouse rescue, Batty Stack, was employed in Cleeves' factory. For him, and for other Volunteers, the prospect of being checked and questioned by the military four times a day was a dangerous one. In addition, there was probably a genuine sense of grievance among Cleeves' employees over the way the military boundaries had been planned. On the Saturday before the strike started, the Cleeves' workers rejected an offer by the authorities to supply them with permits for the coming week. Some authorities have suggested that it was, in fact, a decision by the Cleeves' workers to strike from Monday that forced the hand of the trades council. [6] A confidential police report said the strike had its origins among a number of Sinn Féin members employed at Cleeves' factory. The report went further, and said Sinn Féin had "instigated" the general strike. [7]

On Sunday, 13 April 1919 – Palm Sunday in the Christian liturgy – delegates from the thirty-five unions affiliated to Limerick United Trades and Labour Council met to consider the situation. Their discussions lasted for almost twelve hours, ending at half past eleven that night. In the end, the decision was unanimous. The council decided to call a general strike of all Limerick workers as a protest against the proclamation of the city as a special military area. At a sympathetic printing works in Cornmarket Row, printers worked through the night on a strike proclamation. Within two hours, the city's walls were covered with the notice.

The council elected a strike committee, chaired by the council president, John

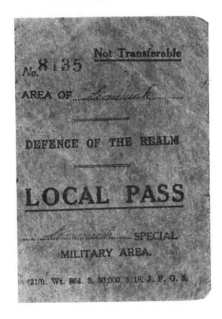

TO WHOM IT MAY CONCERN.
This Pass is Granted to :—

Style or Title
(Mr., Mrs., or Miss) *M.*

SURNAME in Capitals **STEWART**

Christian Names *Henry M.*

Age *41.* Occupation *Jeweller*

Postal Address *104 George St.*
Limerick

Signature of Holder *H m Stewart*

Date of Arrival in Area *Resident*

OFFICIAL STAMP.

APR 1919

PHOTOGRAPH or DESCRIPTION.

Height *5 ft. 3 ins.*
Build *Light*
Hair, Colour *Brown*
Eyes, Colour *Brown*

Issued by *G Williamson*

Rank *2 Lieut*

Station *Limerick*

Date *13/4/19* 191

CONDITIONS

This Pass must be produced for inspection at any time, if required to do so by any Naval or Military Officer, Sailor or Soldier on duty, or Police Officer, or Constable, or any other authorised Person.

This Pass can only be used by a British Subject ordinarily resident in *Limerick*

This Pass may at any time be revoked.

Local pass no. 8153 was issued to Henry Stewart, a jeweller, of 104 George's Street, by 2nd Lieutenant G. Williamson.

No. 8135   Not Transferable

AREA OF *Limerick*

DEFENCE OF THE REALM

LOCAL PASS

Limerick SPECIAL
MILITARY AREA.

(210). Wt. 964. 3. 50,000. 5/18. J. F. G. B.

Cronin, a delegate from the Amalgamated Society of Carpenters. Cronin was an unassuming person, but a great craftsman, having won a gold medal and certificate from the Worshipful Company of Carpenters for proficiency in his trade. Cronin's father had also been president of the trades council and he had followed diligently in his footsteps. The trades council treasurer, the printer James Casey, was elected treasurer of the strike committee. The third officer of the strike committee was an engineering worker named James Carr. Afterwards, in the folklore of Limerick trade unionists, the strike leaders were remembered as "The Three Cs". The strikers also elected subcommittees to take charge of propaganda, finance, food and vigilance – an early indication, perhaps, that they expected a long, rather than a short, strike.

The speedy and efficient way in which the trades' council meeting was organised would seem to underline an element of Sinn Féin influence and support. Certainly, the normal cumbersome methods of consultation with the members of individual affiliated unions were not followed.

On Monday, 14 April 1919 the *Irish Independent* correspondent in Limerick cabled the Dublin office: "Limerick City is on strike. Shops warehouses and factories are closed. No work is being done and no business transacted."[8]

The strikers intended to maintain public utilities like water, gas and electricity, though street lighting was turned off. The strike took the city and its workers by surprise. Nevertheless, almost all workers stayed out and, apart from the post office and the banks, practically every branch of industry stopped and all places of business were closed. The banks did little or no business, but the post office was kept busy by journalists filing copy on Robert Byrne's inquest and the start of the strike. Even the public houses followed the lead.

To avoid the loss of perishable commodities, on the first day of the strike the strike committee allowed employees to work at the bacon and condensed milk factories and the tanneries. The employees of Cleeves' creamery did not turn up for work; instead, they joined in a parade by thousands of workers through streets filled with a holiday atmosphere. Bakers' and butchers' assistants joined the strike. Bread was not obtainable, but it was announced that the bakers would return to work that night, easing initial fears of a food shortage.

In all, more than 14,000 workers were on strike. The *Irish Times* noted: "... nothing doing anywhere, except a Coroner's inquest on the Sinn Féin prisoner, Byrne, who was shot during an attempt to rescue him."[9]

At Kingsbridge Railway Station in Dublin, and at other stations, passengers were refused tickets to Limerick unless they had a permit from the military authorities. Some passengers persisted in making the journey. But the few who arrived in Limerick that Monday morning had considerable difficulty in getting hotel accommodation. Pickets visited all the hotels and ordered them to close their doors. Where visitors were admitted, they were told there could be no

John Cronin, President of Limerick United Trades and Labour Council during the events of April 1919. An American journalist aptly described him as "the father of the baby soviet". Cronin was a highly skilled carpenter, holding a gold medal and certificate for proficiency from the Worshipful Company of Carpenters.

guarantee they would be supplied with food and that supplies could not last beyond the evening. Restaurants, too, were closed.

The 3,000 or so members of the Irish Transport and General Workers' Union were crucial in the strike. Goods for Limerick were not dispatched from the North Wall in Dublin, nor accepted at Kingsbridge, when it became known they would not be handled by the transport workers in Limerick.

The *Independent* reported: "Every thoroughfare in the city is full of people moving about and discussing the situation. There is considerable suppressed excitement, but the people show no disposition to be otherwise than quiet and orderly ... " In a perceptive comment, the newspaper's correspondent wrote: "The strike is in every way complete, and it looks as if there is a possibility of a fierce struggle between organised Labour and the Government." [10]

The *Irish Times* report blamed the Transport Union as the "dominating factor" in encouraging the strike decision. "Associated to some degree with Labour in its action", the newspaper claimed, " is the irresponsible element of Sinn Féin, which, of course, regards the situation as a challenge to British law. The ordinary citizen, however, who has at heart the welfare of the city, and realises how costly will be the strike and the other incidents, is gravely concerned, and anticipates a permanent setback to its trade and commerce. The bill that he will have to meet for the maintenance of the extra police will be a heavy one ... " [11]

The chairman of the strike committee, John Cronin, telegraphed a message to William O'Brien, general secretary of the Irish Labour Party and Trade Union Congress: "General strike here as protest against permit restrictions." [12]

Cronin outlined his assessment of the causes of the strike to newspaper reporters. He said the present industrial situation had arisen out of the tragedy at the workhouse. "The military authorities have seen fit to place Limerick under martial law. In doing that, they have fixed their boundaries inside the city, which makes it necessary for workers to pass in and out to their work. We, as organised workers, refuse to ask them for permits to earn our daily bread, and this strike is a protest against their action. What we want is to have this ban removed so that the workers may have free access to their work in and out of their native city. It is our intention to carry on the strike until this ban is removed. This strike is likely to become more serious." [13]

The strike call threw the Castle authorities, particularly the RIC, into immediate difficulties. Within a half hour of the strike meeting ending, Dublin Castle was being told of the decision. At five minutes to midnight, on the Sunday, District Inspector Craig of the RIC telephoned Dublin. [14] The succinct official record of the telephone message shows that Craig asked for at least 300 extra constables, if possible, to be sent on the first morning train. Alternatively, he would settle for 100 men sent in advance from the Dublin depot. Craig's initial assessment was wise: "The situation looks very serious." [15]

Delegates representing the thirty-five trade unions affiliated to Limerick United Trades and Labour Council in April 1919 – the Limerick "soviet".

The message from Craig prompted a handwritten message to Brigadier-General Joseph Byrne, the inspector-general of the RIC, from the Deputy Inspector-General W.M. Davies, at twenty to two in the morning. [16] The request for 300 police reinforcements was impossible to meet, even with more time available. Davies pointed out that he was reluctant to take men from any of the southern companies, because "there are so many strikes going on elsewhere" – an interesting comment on the level of trade union militancy at the time. [17] Although he knew the military did not intervene in strikes, they would have to do so if disorder arose. This comment suggests this very senior RIC officer did not quite appreciate the extraordinary challenge to authority posed by this particular strike. Indeed, the whole tone of his message to the inspector general is querulous and indecisive.

Forty minutes later, at twenty minutes past two in the morning, a decisive reply came back. [18] Fifty men were to be sent from the depot on the first train. GHQ were to be informed of the policing difficulties. The inspector general's assessment was blunt: "Say to GHQ that as this is no ordinary strike it is presumed instruction will be tonight sent for military to help police." [19]

On the same file in Dublin Castle on the headed notepaper of the Vice Regal Lodge, is a note of two matters decided upon there, that Monday. The first was the text of a communiqué to be telegraphed to Limerick and issued to the Dublin press by the press censor's office. This read: "The public of Limerick are informed that although Limerick has been proclaimed a military area, this in no way prevents the inhabitants from getting their supplies in the ordinary way. If, owing to the wanton action of ill-disposed persons, the inhabitants suffer through lack of the necessities of life, the Government are in no way responsible, and cannot do anything to ameliorate the consequences of such action." [20]

The second decision noted was an instruction to inform the commander in chief that "the Government instructs him to give every possible assistance in the maintenance of Law and Order, especially in view of the fact that Limerick is a military area". [21]

After a slight initial hesitancy, Dublin Castle had recognised the challenge for what it was and made its dispositions to deal with it.

If the lives of Limerick's workers were disrupted by the military regulations, so too were the arrangements of more "respectable" citizens elsewhere. The company secretary of Switzer's department store in Dublin, W.F. Hanna, applied for a permit, saying it was "of extreme importance" that he travel on the Thursday. [22] He wished to be in his native Limerick for the Easter holidays. In the initial period prior to the exact details of the control regulations being published, the Limerick RIC had referred Hanna to the Dublin Metropolitan Police. Indignantly, he pointed out that they professed "complete ignorance – or rather absence of information!". Hanna said that he was a "most law-abiding citizen anxious to mind my own business and no politician". In exasperation he asked the chief secretary for Ireland: "Tell me what I am to do please."

From no. 56, Monson Street, in Lincoln, came a request from Patrick Noonan for a permit to return to Rathkeale, in Co. Limerick, also for the Easter holidays.[23] Noonan explained that he had gone to Lincoln to replace a man who had gone to fight at the Front, being too old himself for military service. He enclosed a newspaper clipping showing he was the author of a telegram to the lord lieutenant of Ireland, from the "loyal Irishmen of Lincoln", expressing deepest sympathy at the sinking of the passenger ferry *Leinster* in October 1918, with a loss of more than 500 lives. The telegram had expressed the hope that the "fiendish outrage which called aloud to Heaven for vengeance would fire the youth of Ireland with the fighting spirit of their race to give, even at the eleventh hour, the final knockout blow to the murderers of our countrymen".

Noonan also enclosed a copy of a reference written for him in 1916 by Major General T.F. Lloyd, colonel the Prince of Wales North Stafford Regiment, at Rathkeale, Co. Limerick. Apart from describing Noonan as a strong Loyalist, the reference said his life had been erratic, taking up various pursuits, among others, correspondent to newspapers, writing especially articles on hunting. "And I never saw anything written by him that was not loyal in every sense of the word," the general commented. Not surprisingly, Noonan got his permit.

Other applicants were referred to their local police. One came from W.F. Enright, a wholesale spirits, cork, butter and general produce merchant in Belfast and another from a person called Walsh in Liverpool. [24]

A week into the strike, the chief secretary for Ireland, the Scot Ian McPherson, received an anonymous letter from Limerick, signed "An Anxious One". [25] The letter began by endorsing a recent speech by McPherson in the House of Commons. Of this speech the parliamentary correspondent of the *British Weekly* – himself an experienced Scottish member of the press gallery – had laconically commented: "This was not the type of speech which Mr McPherson, a Home Ruler, would have liked to deliver, but the man who becomes Chief Secretary for Ireland cannot always do what he likes." [26]

In general, the chief secretary's anonymous Limerick correspondent berated him about the dangers facing the country and the need to maintain morale in the police force. Unless the force was supported, the writer warned, the younger men especially would go over to the rebels, "leaving the country in a bad way and all loyal citizens at the mercy of Rebels who will turn the place into another Russia". This letter was written after a week of the strike and the writer's reference to Russia is of some interest.

The tribulations of the loyal citizens of Limerick even found their way into the hallowed chambers of Buckingham Palace. On the fourth day of the strike, Mrs Anna Worrall of Catherine Place, in Limerick, wrote to his Majesty King

George V. [27] Mrs Worrall wrote to ask a favour of the King, knowing she said, that since the war he was "only too ready to hear all about his subjects". She hoped the letter would not be thrown in the wastepaper basket but would be given to the king himself.

Mrs Worrall's request was to have the military tanks removed from the Wellesley Bridge (now called Sarsfield Bridge) to the borough boundary at the Workhouse Cross in Co. Clare. This, she pointed out, would allow the men and women workers to go freely to Cleeves' factory. The general strike, she complained, "makes it hard for everyone". The grocers and bakers were the only shops allowed to open, from 2 pm to 5 pm.

"They are all 'Sinn Féiners'," she declared, "but the Government ought to think a little of us few loyal subjects and it is no use making them more bitter than they are, nor do we want bloodshed here over it. No one knows I am writing to your Majesty. Will you send orders to Head Quarters in Dublin by return and grant the request I ask."

King George's private secretary passed the letter to Dublin Castle. District Inspector Rodwell reported from Limerick that Mrs Worrall was a most respectable and loyal old lady, but was considered "slightly eccentric". [28] She frequently visited her brother, the well-known auctioneer Fitt, who lived on the Ennis Road and had to show her pass when crossing the Wellesley Bridge. Laconically, Rodwell noted: "She probably does not like doing this."

Other concerned citizens were expressing their views too on the effects of the proclamation. Limerick corporation adopted a resolution criticising the allocation of extra police [29] and the ever-active P.J. Kelly, resident magistrate, convened a meeting of his colleagues to consider the state of the city. [30]

Now the powder keg had exploded, and the pieces could never be put back together again.

CHAPTER SEVEN

Food, Money and Newspapers

"Limerick, famous all over the world for the quality of its bacon, will at
the present rate soon be without the morning rasher."
The Irish Independent, 19 April 1919

The first, and most fundamental, task facing the strikers was that of literally
feeding Limerick's 38,000 inhabitants.

The suddenness with which the strike was called, and became effective, meant
that rich and poor alike were taken unawares. On the first Monday of the strike
there was panic over the continuity of food supply and an *Irish Independent*
headline warned of "The Peril of Famine". [1] That evening, in its first major
assertion of power, the strike committee ordered the bakers to resume work. In
its report on this development, the *Irish Times* for the first time referred to the
committee as the local "soviet", though it is not quite clear from the context
whether the reference was sarcastic or not. [2] In any event, however, the report
indicates that even on the first day of the strike it was being referred to in some
quarters as a "soviet".

After the soviet's order, crowds of women and children lined up outside the
bakeries early on Tuesday morning in the hope of getting bread and it was handed
out to them fresh from the ovens.

Describing the shortage of food on the first day of the soviet, the *Irish Times*
waxed lyrical: "In this land of plenty, in the heart of the Golden Vale, it is not
easy for the stranger to procure food. The bakeries are closed and the butchers'
shops are shut, with the result that the hotel larders are scantily stocked. Biscuits
and cheese were never so appetising as today, when they sustained many a weary
traveller through a trying time. Milk, however, could hardly be had, though there
are creameries everywhere. The visitor from Dublin, of course, did not mind the
shortage of butter, but he did miss his margarine ... " [3]

On that first day, other foodstuffs, potatoes for example, were running
alarmingly low, and fresh meat was impossible to obtain. [7] All the public houses
rigidly enforced the order to close. Even the most favoured customers could not
buy a drink anywhere and the *Irish Independent* wryly noted in heavy black type:

"Limerick is an absolutely dry city."[4]

If there were no public houses, at least the citizens still had the cinemas for entertainment. Some of these were glad to open with notices outside the door: "Open by authority of the Strike Committee."[5] But there was a plaintive letter of protest to the *Irish Independent* about the closure of the Limerick Free Library. The writer, "Munchin", admitted that the general strike was in defence of the public, but he warned the new "powers-that-be that in striving for the public rights they should not trample on public privileges".[6] The public park, where the library was situated, had not been closed. So, "Munchin" enquired, if it was possible to look after the recreation of the body, why not recreation of the mind? This, he argued, was especially true when "time hangs heavily on many men's hands, and newspapers, even for money are hard to get".

The soviet's control of the city's business ran deep. Drapery and boot shops were not opened, so that anyone needing a collar and tie had to get it surreptitiously from a friendly proprietor, or get a soviet permit! An American journalist staying in the city had to make an eloquent appeal to a soviet sub committee for permission to buy a shirt.[7] Even chemists' shops were confined to limited Sunday opening hours.

However, from early on, the Soviet claimed to have the food situation well in hand. They sat in session in the Mechanics' Institute from early morning until late at night, carrying out their arrangements with thoroughness and attention to detail. They issued hundreds – another report says "sheaves" – of permits to shops to open and supply foodstuffs, between two and five o'clock in the afternoon.[8]

The soviet strictly controlled the price of food. They issued posters throughout the city showing a list of retail prices for essential foodstuffs. The posters warned that drastic measures would be taken to prevent profiteering. Pickets wearing distinctive badges patrolled the streets. They ensured no shops opened without permission and that they were not overcrowded during the hours of opening.

In general, the provision merchants acted in harmony with the soviet and they kept prices at normal levels. After a week, the *Independent* commented: "It is certainly a remarkable tribute to the skill and organisation of the Strike Committee that while there has been a general suspension of all branches of industry in the city now for seven days, there has been no scarcity of food."[9] Large purchases were discouraged, so hoarding was prevented.

Given that the *Irish Times* was always critical of the strike, its grudgingly favourable comments on the food situation on the same date are an interesting indication of the soviet's effectiveness. In a comment on the food supply, the newspaper said: " ... though it is daily diminishing, it should not be thought there is immediate danger of serious distress ... the people there are, therefore, well supplied with milk, and they also have fair supplies of other necessaries."[10]

It would be wrong to give the impression, though, that the soviet's relations with the city's business people were entirely harmonious. For many of them, believers in the rights of property, it must have been galling to have to take orders from a group of mere workers and to hear John Cronin declare: "The necessary steps have been taken to ensure a sufficient supply of food for the people ..." [11]

After the first week of the strike, the *Irish Times* found some business people who were "suffering considerable inconvenience and loss as a result of closing their establishments, and they would be glad to see the strike ended and the old order of things restored." [12] They may have been among the traders who, at that time, threatened to open their premises in spite of soviet opposition. On the second Monday of the soviet, some shopkeepers did, indeed, do that but they were punished the following day by having their opening hour delayed.

No deliveries of bread were allowed to shops or private homes – everyone had to buy their supplies directly from the bakeries. Farmers from outside the city, normally dependent on bread carts for deliveries, had to come in to collect their supplies. As the *Independent* noted: " ... it was no uncommon spectacle to see an aged peasant driving an ass and cart laden with bread through the streets". [13]

Throughout the life of the soviet, the problem of bread supplies remained crucial. Obviously, it was closely linked to supplies of flour, but also to supplies of coal, since the bakery ovens were coal-fired. To ensure supplies of flour, the soviet gave permission for the unloading of 7,000 tons of Canadian grain at the docks.

It appears that in some instances the soviet tried to requisition food supplies. Dublin Castle records note a file about a demand to Cleeves' factory for "butter etc. required by the Transport Union"! [14]

Limerick's food problems offered the first opportunity for those who sympathised with the strike outside the city to give practical help. A Catholic priest, Fr Kennedy of Ennis, Co. Clare, helped to organise the farmers in the south east of the county, near the city, to supply food to Limerick. The soviet food committee was divided into two sections – one to receive food and the other to distribute it. Food depots were set up in Thomondgate, on the Clare side of the Shannon, because it was outside the controlled area. Four city councillors controlled the collection and distribution of food through four depots established by the soviet. [15]

The Clare farmers sent potatoes, milk, eggs, butter, tea, sugar and homemade bread into the depots and these were sold at prices considerably below the market value. Through a combination of circumstances, the people of Limerick suffered no shortage of milk and it was available at a very cheap price. Because of the closure of Cleeves' condensed milk factory, the farmers found themselves with supplies on hand. This was sold to the city's poor at three pence or four pence a quart, compared with the usual price of seven pence. The maximum price set by the soviet was four pence.

Towards the end of the soviet's existence, the supply of food from Co. Clare received ecclesiastical approval at a high level. At Sunday masses in the diocese of Killaloe, the priests appealed to the congregations to help Limerick with food supplies, saying they did so with the sanction and approval of the bishop, Dr Fogarty. [16] There was a generous response, including one gift of twenty tons of potatoes.

Other more unorthodox methods were used to bring in food. In a memoir of the soviet, the trades council treasurer, James Casey, recalls that relays of boats with muffled oars were successfully used to run food and other supplies through the blockade. [17] On other occasions, Casey recalled, the funeral hearses from the Union Hospital, outside the military cordon, did not always contain corpses!

Cork and other centres offered to send food, as did a number of British trade unions. Farmers and shopkeepers outside Limerick who wished to send gifts of food were asked to send them by rail to the city, consigned to the "Food Commission, Mechanics' Hall, Limerick". Any food received in this way was to be stocked in wholesale stores under the commission's control and then distributed to shopkeepers who were willing to recognise the authority of the strike committee. If necessary, the commission would open supplementary retail shops.

The quantity of food sent by farmers, especially from Co. Clare, in support of what was clearly a Labour agitation raises intriguing questions in view of the many strikes involving farm labourers at that time. Not all farmers were willing donors to the strikers' stockpile of food. A veteran of the soviet, Dan Clancy, recalled an incident that occurred in the "Little Market", off Robert Street, when the strikers compelled the farmers to give away food for "half nothing". [18] As the police stood by helplessly, the strikers ordered the farmers from the market. Clancy recalled sardonically: "They all flocked to the Republic." Since the normal methods and outlets for disposing of their produce were closed, many farmers decided to make a patriotic virtue out of necessity. But the involvement of Fr Kennedy, in Ennis, suggests a degree of organisation by Sinn Féin and its sympathisers, and of course, one cannot rule out feelings of genuine nationalism on the part of some farmers.

Pig and cattle fairs were seriously disrupted by the strike. The April Munster Fair, held in the second week of the strike, had no more than one-tenth of the usual supply of cattle. Buyers were few and little business was done. The pig-buyers were seriously affected by a prohibition on the killing of about 200 pigs which had been bought during the first two days of the soviet. Bacon supplies were exhausted in some of the shops. "Limerick," the *Irish Independent* noted, "famous all over the world for the quality of its bacon will, at the present rate, soon be without the morning rasher." [19] The military themselves were forced to make special arrangements to bring supplies by train to Limerick from Dublin and Cork.

After food, fuel was next in importance. The soviet allowed coal and coke merchants to open between ten and five o'clock, but supplies were running alarmingly low, and very limited quantities were given out. In general, the coal merchants were hostile and refused to open their yards. Rather than force a violent confrontation, however, the soviet reluctantly accepted this. But the soviet warned the coal merchants they were not to co-operate with the military by supplying them with fuel, nor should they supply customers who had obtained military permits.

After a week, the cautious *Irish Times* commented that "while the food question seems to have been solved for the present, the question of money is causing anxiety to many families ... " [20] The majority of trade unions seemed to have been prepared to pay their members strike pay for the duration of the soviet, but a key trade union like the National Union of Railwaymen made it clear that it would not. In addition, at the end of the first week, while outside food supplies were readily forthcoming, little money had been received.

Faced with this prospect, the soviet took one of its most historic and, indeed, spectacular decisions. This was to print its own currency, in denominations of one, five and ten shillings. The decision does not seem to have been based on any ideological considerations, but was a straightforward pragmatic response to a shortage of money.

Tom Johnson, treasurer of the Trade Union Congress, who had been sent by the executive to liaise with the Limerick strikers, said the security for the notes, in the first place, would be the stocks of food being presented free by outsider sympathisers, then the financial support and integrity of the workers of Limerick, backed by the national feeling. [21] Later, the currency was backed by the trades council and the Trade Union Congress itself and accepted by approved shops. A list was compiled of merchants and shopkeepers who were willing to give credit to the trades council.

Johnson said the notes issue was "sound finance" and was a sign the strike could be prolonged. [22] The *Irish Times* saw the currency more as a type of promissory note or food voucher and therefore as "a sign of growing financial weakness ... The impression, therefore, is gaining ground that the crisis has passed and that the close of the week will synchronise with the close of the strike." [23]

There has been controversy over whether some notes were counterfeited. In an article in the *Irish Times* in May 1969, Jim Kemmy used illustrations of two notes denominated as one shilling and five shillings. The illustrations were copied by the *Irish Times* from the publication *Fifty Years of Liberty Hall*, edited

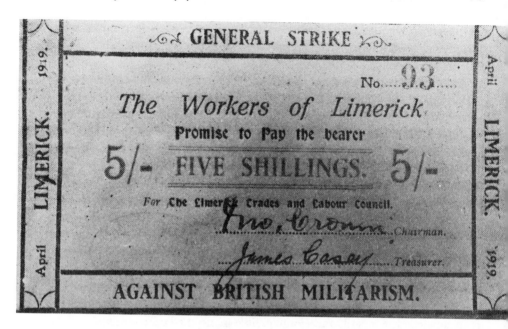

The decision to issue its own currency, in the denominations of a shilling, five shillings and ten shillings, marked out the Limerick soviet as a unique event in Irish or British Labour history. Eventually, the soviet redeemed the entire issue, although there were later allegations of forgery.

by Cathal O'Shannon. Subsequently, in a letter to the newspaper, a son of John Cronin – Jeremiah – challenged the authenticity of his father's signature on the notes reproduced. The signature in the illustration accompanying his letter was certainly different from the earlier illustration. But Jeremiah Cronin offered no explanation or theory as to how the difference in signatures arose. Opinion differs as to whether the notes were forgeries, or whether someone signed them in John Cronin's name with his delegated authority. After the strike was over, surplus money was sought as souvenirs and this too might account for the forgeries.

A sub-committee of the propaganda committee was responsible for the printing and issuing of the currency and, not unexpectedly, the sub-committee mainly consisted of accounts staff from large firms like Cleeves, the bacon factories, the flour mills and the corporation. According to James Casey, when the notes were ultimately redeemed, a small surplus remained in a fund that had been subscribed to by sympathisers in all parts of Ireland. [24]

Whatever the original motivation for the issuing of currency that decision alone places Limerick in a unique position in Labour history. At the time the significance of the currency was not lost on socialists. At the annual conference of the Independent Labour Party, in Britain, "Councillor Cradford of Edinburgh said that they ought to do something to encourage the 'Limerick soviet' which had got over its financial difficulties by the issue of a paper currency of its own. He would like to see the working-class of this country do the same. In spite of what Mr Ramsay McDonald had said, the 'Limerick soviet' was the first working-class soviet on practical lines established in these islands ... " [25]

Transport and communications were important enough to merit the setting up of a permits committee under the charge of four city councillors. The carters who worked at conveying perishable goods displayed printed cards, sometimes on the horse's bridle: "Working under the authority of the Strike Committee." [26] The committee issued permits to merchants to obtain and carry commodities like coal, butter and flour from the railway station to shops. Doctors, chauffeurs and car drivers got permits when necessary. The only vehicles allowed on the streets were those owned by people who had appeared before the permits committee. Any other cars were immediately ordered off the streets by the workers' patrols. In all, the soviet issued thousands of transport permits.

An American army officer arrived by train and got the necessary military permit to enter the city. He intended to visit relatives outside Limerick but he could not induce any of the hackney carriers to drive him to his destination. After a time he appeared before the permits committee and got permission to travel. He delivered a spirited speech, in which he promised to expose British rule in Ireland when he returned to the United States. "I guess," he concluded, "it is some puzzle to know who rules in these parts. You have to get a military permit to get in, and be brought before a committee to get a permit to leave." [27]

All in all, the soviet and its sub-committees carried off the job of feeding and regulating the lives of 38,000 Limerick citizens with remarkable effectiveness. Not a single case of looting was reported, nor did a single court case come up for hearing at the petty sessions. After eight days in the city, an American journalist commented that he had not seen one person under the influence of drink nor a single disorderly incident.[28] Given human nature, however, that generalised assertion seems unlikely to be true. But in several reports, various newspapers commented favourably on the peace and good order prevailing in the city and the absolute control exercised by the soviet and its "ministers".

But the name of Limerick, and its remarkable achievements, were soon to receive worldwide news coverage due to the fortuitously planned arrival there of a celebrated traveller and adventurer.

CHAPTER EIGHT

The World Watches

"We are spectators today of a very bold and candid experiment
in Irish Syndicalism."
Irish Times editorial on "The Strike at Limerick" , 23 April 1919.

In April 1919 Major J C P Wood intended to fly the Atlantic from east to west, using Limerick as his departure point, to win a £10,000 prize offered by the London *Daily Mail*. Major Wood never quite made it to Limerick in his attempt, but his plan did ensure the presence in the city, from the very start of the soviet, of a large international press corps. Expecting to cover one major news story, these journalists found another one under their noses and cabled their reports diligently around the world.

The strides made in aviation during World War I meant there was considerable post-war interest in the commercial and other possibilities offered by air travel. In early 1919 the air ministry still controlled the air and prohibited civilian flying though it was announced that this would resume on May 1. The newspapers speculated eagerly on the changes the establishment of civilian air links would bring. Schemes had been put forward for a service between London and Cape Town, and London to Egypt had already been flown. Hull chamber of commerce was supporting a scheme for a service to Scandinavia across the North Sea. There was talk of linking Ireland to the North of England and Wales by a service to Liverpool.

But, overshadowing all of these proposals was the challenge of the unconquered Atlantic. The London *Daily Mail* offered a prize of £10,000 to the first aviator to cross the Atlantic, and the manufacturers of "State Express" cigarettes were prepared to add 2,000 guineas to it. Six contestants came forward to try for the prize.

The big problem facing the flyers was the weather. "Like Cleopatra," the *Irish Times* commented in an editorial, "the Atlantic weather has an infinite variety. Anticyclones drift hither and thither above the Ocean's broad expanse, and the airman may encounter seventeen different brands of weather in his flight in as many hundreds of miles. The pioneer of the crossing will owe his success partly to daring, partly to skill, but most of all, perhaps, to luck." [1]

By flying westward from Ireland, Major Wood was facing into the prevailing winds, increasing the estimated flight time from twenty to thirty hours. But he would have the advantage of spending most of his flying time in daylight. By following the line of the Shannon to Loop Head, in Co. Clare, the major was positioning himself for a direct flight line across the Atlantic to St. John's in Newfoundland, a distance of around 1,750 miles. Another not inconsiderable advantage was the much greater likelihood in a westward flight of making landfall in North America, whereas an eastward flight might miss the British Isles altogether if the plane was blown off course. The *Daily Mail* rules stipulated that an eastward flight had to touch land in either Ireland or Britain.

The major's planned departure caused great excitement in Limerick. A seventy acre field at Bawnmore, some miles outside the city, was prepared for the flight, with a huge whitewashed cross marked in the centre of the flying ground. Bawnmore had no hangars, but it had been temporarily used before the war by the Royal Flying Corps and it was close to the Shannon, an admirable navigational guide. It had the advantage too of being an elevated site, and the flight would not be delayed by a boggy runway if the weather was bad.

Six hundred gallons of fuel were stored in Limerick in preparation for the flight and it was speculated that the military might move it to Bawnmore, if the carters refused to carry it because of the strike. But this proved not to be necessary. Sir Stephen Quinn, one of the local notables involved in assisting the major's preparations, went to see the strike committee. John Cronin said that they had no objection to the major starting his flight from Limerick, provided he admitted he was starting there by permission of the strikers. Sir Stephen said he would convey the message to Wood, and subsequently the fuel was moved to Bawnmore. [2] The soviet also granted permits to drivers to bring press reporters and photographers to the take-off point.

Wood planned to make his flight, with his navigator Captain Wyllie, in a 4,800lb Short-Rolls Royce machine called "The Shamrock". The idea was that as the fuel was consumed the plane would become lighter, and it could stay in the air for up to forty-two hours at speeds of between eighty-five and ninety-five miles an hour. Both airmen wore a complicated type of heated clothing. Wires ran through their combination suits from a small dynamo operated by a propeller, and with the flick of a switch, they were able to heat themselves electrically. On the left side of the plane was a row of thermos flasks filled with hot coffee and a couple of flasks of brandy.

Wood and Wyllie proposed to take plenty of sandwiches and tablet preparations of chocolate, fruit cake and meat. These, *The Times* noted, were in case they were blown a long way off course and had "to land in some out-of-the-way part of the American continent". [3]

After several postponements because of bad weather, excitement in Limerick reached fever pitch as people awaited the major's arrival from England. On the second day of the strike, crowds of people went to Bawnmore in anticipation of his arrival. Two days later, there was another exodus from the city by car and bicycle. No less than a score of cinema newsreel photographers prepared stands to get the best vantage point and stills photographers took up positions on walls or on the adjoining hills. There were journalists there from all parts of the world, including a large American contingent with waiting cars on standby to carry special telegraph messengers with express dispatches. At one stage, a military scouting plane hovered over the crowds.

All eyes strained eastwards, towards the Silvermines and Galtee Mountains, for the first glimpse of "The Shamrock". But it was not to be seen. After four hours flying, Major Wood's plane cut out over the Irish Sea and he was forced to ditch a short distance from the Anglesey coast. A group of picnickers who saw the plane in difficulties put a small boat out to sea and picked up the plane's two occupants. Wood made this laconic comment to one of the rescuers: "Atlantic flight biffed!" [4]

Wood had left the Royal Flying Corps aerodrome at Eastchurch, Isle of Sheppey, in beautiful weather and in good spirits. Over the past eleven days, three engines had been tested before one was fitted permanently. To find eight reliable sparking plugs, 400 were tested. A Church of England chaplain prayed "God Speed!" for the flyers, and all the aerodrome hands gave hearty cheers as the major took off.

Although Major Wood's adventure was only one of several transatlantic flights planned that week, his was the only one to go westwards, and he was actually the first competitor into the air in the *Daily Mail* race. In Newfoundland, flight pioneers like Hawker, Morgan and the Australian Raynham grappled with snowstorms, which prevented take-off. A journalist asked Raynham why, unlike other contestants, his plane did not carry a life raft. He replied that this was due to the fact that he intended to cross the Atlantic, not to fall into it! [5]

All along the west coast of Ireland preparations were made to keep a look-out for the first plane to make land, and to convey the news to London. The *Irish Times* said the first "watcher of the skies" to catch a glimpse of the plane would be a humble actor in one of the most notable events in the history of the world, whether fisherman, coastguard or village curate going his daily round. On 15 June 1919, the aviators John William Alcock and Arthur Whitten Brown landed their plane in a boggy field near Clifden, in Co. Galway, and claimed the place in history that Wood and the others had so desperately sought.

Apart from bringing news of the soviet to a worldwide readership, the presence of the international press corps had an added advantage for John Cronin and his colleagues. The foreign journalists were able to file their copy through the American cable station at Valentia Island, in Co. Kerry, and so could avoid censorship or interference with their material by the British authorities. On the other hand, all reports sent, and published, in Irish and British newspapers were still subject to official censorship – another one of the powers exercised under the Defence of the Realm Act. Indeed, many contemporary newspapers reports on Limerick carry the legend "Passed by the Official Censor".

Among the foreign journalists based in Limerick at the time were Mr Morris of the Associated Press of America, whose reports were syndicated to 750 American newspapers, Ruth Russell of the *Chicago Tribune*, who wrote a book called *What's the Matter with Ireland?*, and Mr Philmore of the Paris *Le Matin*. In its edition of 15 April 1919, *Le Matin* carried a short report on what it called "A Political Strike at Limerick". Each evening, the soviet propaganda committee held briefings for the foreign journalists, indicating the sophistication with which they undertook their task.

But, relations between the soviet and the press did not always run smoothly. One British pictorial daily carried a paragraph describing "Limerick's Comic Opera Strike". When the newspaper reached Limerick, a picket was immediately sent to the hotel where the offending correspondent was staying. In less than half an hour, he was standing before the strike committee. Pale and trembling, he explained that the heading had been written by a sub-editor and that he could not be held responsible. The committee warned him that if anything further detrimental to the strike appeared in his newspaper, they would cut off light, food and water from his hotel. The warning had the desired effect.

The London correspondent of a newspaper called the *Cork Constitution* claimed the strikers were trying to intimidate correspondents. [6] He alleged threats were being made to reporters if the reports which appeared did not suit the views of the strike leaders. An English news agency alleged that post office staff in Limerick were scrutinising reporters' cables and that "any journalist who told the truth was a marked man". However, some days later, British and American journalists repudiated allegations that they were being intimidated in their work by sympathisers of the soviet. A letter refuting the allegation was sent to the Limerick postmaster by the special correspondents of the *Daily News*, *Daily Express*, *Daily Chronicle*, *Manchester Guardian* and *Daily Mail*. As representatives of the British press, they said, they desired to dissociate themselves from this reflection on the integrity of the Limerick post office staff. At the same time, they wanted to thank the postmaster and his staff for the great courtesy they had shown them during the strike.

The *Manchester Guardian* was severely critical of the government's use of what it termed one of the most drastic provisions of the DORA regulations against Limerick.[7] It called for the attention of parliament. The scheduling of special military areas under DORA was intended purely as a safeguard against

German espionage during the war in great naval and military centres such as the north of Scotland and Dover. The permit system was used only to detain suspects. The *Guardian* concluded: "It was certainly never contemplated as an instrument for the punishment of Irish districts in which casual outrages had been committed."

In another comment, the *Guardian*, obviously enjoying the government's discomfiture, pointed out that the workers of Limerick in setting up a "provisional government" were merely following the example of Sir Edward Carson and his supporters who had blocked Home Rule for Ireland by threatening to establish the same in Ulster.[8]

Understandably, other British newspapers were more critical of the soviet itself, of the motives behind it and of what it might lead to. The *Times* said Ireland had never been more prosperous and the bulk of the community objected very strongly to the wanton creation of industrial strife.[9] The newspaper said any general strike could not last long without funds, and the Limerick workers were looking to England for help. "But we fancy that English working men have other uses for their money, now none too plentiful, and will hardly be willing to put it into a country which has grown affluent during the War", the *Times* speculated. The newspaper consoled itself with the belief that there was in reality no country where the doctrines of syndicalism were less likely to obtain a firm hold than Ireland.

The *Morning Post* took a serious view of the events in Limerick.[10] The *Post* claimed Sinn Féin was secretly conducting affairs according to a definite plan. "When the local Soviets have obtained possession and control of the local resources Sinn Féin will thus control the greater part of Ireland ... Unless the government intervene, local control by Sinn Féin will include what is most important of all – control of the roads and railways." The *Morning Post*, therefore, called for tougher Government measures. The *Daily Chronicle* too was convinced the strike was part of a Sinn Féin campaign.[11]

From Limerick, the special correspondent of the *Daily Express* sent these graphic words: "The city is as much in military occupation as Cologne ... There is nothing comparable with the situation today, outside certain Continental European countries. The leadership mean to win, and it certainly seems as if the workers of Ireland were with them ... I have witnessed many strikes in England but never one bearing any resemblance to this. It is the grand slam, and it suggests possibilities on which it is not pleasant to ponder."[12]

The *Westminster Gazette* was fairly measured in its comments.[13] It said the transport workers were credited with the plan of attempting a general strike in Ireland, but it was admitted that this idea required financial support from Britain. The newspaper ruled that out as a possibility, and it said the government had taken measures and was "very wisely allowing the strike to blow off steam".

The *Pall Mall Gazette* said it was not sure that the military measures out of which the strike arose were free from a provocative element, but the strike was for political and not for industrial purposes and therefore "without justification from the standpoint of constitutional Labour". [14]

In Belfast, the Unionist *News Letter* saw the direction of government policy as being in capable hands and it commended General Griffin's "tactful" behaviour. [15] The *Irish News*, a long-time supporter of the now declining Irish National Party, was scathing in its criticism of the strike. It denounced it as a "picturesque form of protest, but it will not worry Dublin Castle in the slightest degree ... ", while Limerick itself would suffer severely if the strike continued for many days. [16] "What could be gained," the *Irish News* asked, "even if the people remained idle for a week, a fortnight or a month? Many traders and a few manufacturers might be beggared, thousands of wage-earners would sacrifice their incomes, thousands would go hungry, but no soldiers' rations would be curtailed to the extent of an ounce." The voice of old-fashioned Belfast nationalism concluded: "The wisdom of those who invented and promoted this costly kind of protest against an unjust Castle 'proclamation' must be regarded as more than questionable."

While the news reporting of the *Irish Independent* on the soviet was often colourful, and seemed fair, the paper's only editorial on the matter was a curious mixture of criticism of the authorities balanced by criticism of the strikers and, above all, a fear that matters might escalate into a general strike. [17] Given the conservative nature of its proprietors' politics, the *Independent* was happy to see the government challenged, but not by a movement led by organised labour. Down that road lay dangers for the nationalist middle-classes themselves.

The *Independent* began on a stirring note: "Militarism has been crushed in Prussia only to be set up in Ireland in a way that is a negation of civil liberty." The authorities were going too far; the ordinary criminal law was enough to deal with outrages or raids. Putting an entire city under practically the same rule as if it were in a war zone did not capture and punish the evil-doers. A whole community was punished and subjected to needless and wanton inconvenience. The resulting resentment lessened the chances of catching the perpetrators of crimes. "Limerick, a singularly crimeless city before the unfortunate occurrence of a few weeks ago, is besieged and treated as if all its inhabitants were diabolical criminals," the editorial complained.

In a neat twist of argument, the paper reminded the authorities that brutal and savage murders were not uncommon in Britain and there had been serious riots there, but no city or district "on the other side of the Channel" had been put under military rule.

Turning to the workers, the *Independent* thought their action "hasty" but felt sure that while Irish nationalists differed as to the wisdom of the action the majority of them would sympathise with its objects. But the paper would not countenance an escalation of Limerick into a national general strike, saying it would be "productive of very serious results for the country as a whole".

The Limerick strikers had, unthinkingly, played into the government's hands and instead of embarrassing the authorities were simply increasing the loss, inconvenience and suffering of the people at large. In any event, the *Independent* pointed out, Ulster, or a large part of it, would not respond to any call for a national strike, "so that the loss and inconvenience would fall exclusively on Nationalist Ireland".

The *Irish Times* devoted three editorials to the soviet. On the morning after the rescue of Robert Byrne the newspaper had three targets in its editorial sights. [18] Seizing on the phrase "no arrests have been made", the *Irish Times* said that that sentence had been the burden of all the recent stories of outrage. In its view, a state of terrorism prevailed throughout the country. The government owed an urgent duty to the people to strengthen the arm of the law to assure decent men of such protection as would embolden them to help it to save their country's peace and honour. If the crown forces were insufficient, they must be increased; if the law was inadequate, the editorial continued, the government must seek new powers from parliament.

The *Irish Times* then turned to two other sources for support. They appealed to "the acknowledged leaders of the Sinn Féin movement" to express their horror for the crime of murder and they called on the Roman Catholic church to "enlist all its tremendous sanctions on the side of morality and law". Individual churchmen had denounced individual crimes with fitting fervour, but the hour demanded nothing less than a solemn protest and warning from the whole body of the hierarchy.

A week later, after the first day of the soviet had ended, the *Irish Times* returned to the theme of "Lawlessness in Ireland". [19] The teachings of Sinn Féin, the *Irish Times* said, had created a far-reaching atmosphere of sedition. It had got into the heads of thousands of young Irishmen who thought it was a fine thing to give the maximum of trouble to authority – and the Irishman was the most ingenious maker of trouble in the world.

Referring specifically to Limerick, the newspaper conceded that the measures taken were pure coercion and furnished no remedy for the root-causes of nationalist discontent. But they were not intended to be, the editorial pointed out. The Government's first duty was "the maintenance of the King's authority and the protection of life and property... So long as crime and violence can be committed with impunity throughout large areas of Ireland, the Government must suppress them forcibly."

The *Irish Times* turned again to "moderate" nationalists and the Catholic church. The government's actions, it argued, were an unsatisfactory substitute

THE WORKER'S BULLETIN

Vol. 1. No. 3. (New Series)   *April 18th, 1919.*

Remember Limerick.

Another day of the Big Strike has passed away, and the Strike Committee were kept working at full pressure. Messages of support arrive constantly from all quarters, and as time goes on determination grows.

Profiteers.

A few cases of shops attempting to use the present crisis in order to profiteer and in under-weight was promptly suppressed by our pickets. We promise full exposure of any more such attempts in the Bulletin.

Up Thomondgate.

Our friends across the river are playing their part, and have set up a Food Depot from which they will send supplies to the besieged.

Our besiegers are trying to spread the idea that famine is imminent, but the Strike Committee have made full arrangements, and can now guarantee an ample supply of food stuffs. Hunger has no great terror for Limerick and we will show that we can suffer privation if necessary in the cause of freedom. All who are anxious to help should place their services at the disposal of the Food Control Committee, Mechanics' Institute.

Arrival of Tom Johnson.

Tom Johnson arrived from the National Executive of the Irish Trades Union Congress last night, and had a prolonged interview with the Strike Committee. He expressed his admiration at the lightning move of the Big Strike, and paid a tribute to the magnificent spirit of Limerick. He got full information of the whole position, and gave most encouraging reports of the situation in Dublin and elsewhere. We can assure the citizens that Limerick will not be left to fight the workers' battle unaided. For obvious reasons we cannot give further details, as our plans will be our plans, and the fight must go on.

Significant Reports.

A surprise awaits our military autocrats, who, in their blind and unjustified thirst for revenge on innocent people, have overstepped the mark.

'Tis true that British soldiers have been used in the past to do the dirty work of their capitalist bosses; men who enlisted " to fight for Small Nationalities " have been forced to dragoon their fellow-workers—of course in the interests of freedom, moryah! We wonder if anyone ever heard of rifles being turned the wrong way—we mean, of course, the butt-end to the front. Men like to fight men on equal terms, but when it comes to starving and dragooning one's own class, especially women and tender babes, in the interests of autocracy, it may become a different story.

"The Workers' Bulletin" began simply enough, as a single-page propaganda leaflet. But it ran for at least seven issues and in its final format was very much like a local newspaper of the time in format and content.

for a public opinion that would discourage, denounce and expose violence. "We have no such public opinion today because the leaders of one half of Nationalist Ireland are preachers of sedition, and the leaders of the other half are unwilling, or afraid, to open their mouths." The Roman Catholic bishop of Ross, Dr Kelly, had told "his people the plain truth in his sermon on Palm Sunday". The bishop's fear of "the influence of Irish Bolshevism on the religious authority of the Church" seemed to the *Irish Times* to be so well-founded that the silence of the church as a whole filled the editorial writer with surprise.

Just over a week later, the *Irish Times* devoted its final editorial to "The Strike at Limerick", again using the term "soviet" to describe the way the city was being run. [20] The paper saw the attempts to extend the strike to all of Ireland as a "very bold and candid experiment in Irish Syndicalism". But, taking the same view as the *Independent*, the *Irish Times* said there could not be a national strike because "the sturdy and well-organised labour of north-east Ulster will have nothing to say to it. The truth is that Syndicalism and Bolshevism, with their common motto 'What is yours is mine, and what is mine is my own' never will make any headway in this country. In our farming classes the sense of property is as sacred and strong as in the French. Our middle-classes are hard-working individualists. The bulk of Irish labour, both urban and rural, is restless today, but it is shrewd and intelligent."

More specifically on Limerick, the *Irish Times* hoped the Irish people would be sobered and instructed by the story. "We are not sorry General Griffin decided to give the local soviet a free hand." The soviet, the paper argued, had inflicted "more arbitrary restrictions on individual liberties than were ever attempted by Prussian bureaucracy in its mightiest hour".

This time, there was no reference to the Catholic church's influence, but there was another appeal to moderate nationalists: "The agitation is a challenge to British government in Ireland, against which some Irishmen have worked themselves up to a pitch so mad that they would prefer a bloodstained and bankrupt Bolshevism to an Ireland safe and progressive under British rule. Today, however, these men are acting with the tacit consent – though not, we are convinced with the genuine approval – of a majority of Irish Nationalists. The Nationalist Press does not criticise them. No Nationalist organisation has warned the country against their schemes."

Despite that type of critical comment, the people of Limerick were eager for news during the soviet. When the morning mail train arrived, there was a wild rush for the Dublin morning papers and in twenty minutes they were all bought up. Demand for newspapers was so great that, in the evening, the newsboys were selling the *Herald* at three pence to six pence a copy.

The soviet allowed the local Limerick papers to publish one issue a week carrying an imprint in bold type: "Published by Permission of the Strike

Committee." But the soviet itself also went into the newspaper business, publishing a daily news sheet called *The Worker's Bulletin.*

The *Bulletin* started simply enough, as a single sheet, more like a propaganda leaflet. But it ran for at least seven issues, and in its final editions was very much like a local newspaper of the time in content and format. Each edition of the *Bulletin* carried in bold type the legend: "Issued by the Limerick Proletariat." It was a clever mixture of news reports and propaganda leavened by some humour and it represented a fine achievement by the propaganda committee.

Another initiative of that committee was their reply to the government's statement disclaiming any responsibility for hardship caused to the citizens. The military posted typewritten copies of the statement in the streets but because they could not commandeer a printing works, they were severely handicapped in the propaganda war. The soviet's reply was that they would rely on the old and proud traditions of Limerick to suffer any difficulties patiently.

So, after a week, the soviet had succeeded better than either its friends or enemies could have imagined. Food, travel, finances and propaganda all appeared to be under control. The scene was set for the first major physical confrontation with the British military and for General Griffin's first divisive concession.

CHAPTER NINE

Confrontation

"The whole scene made a remarkable picture. The crowds on the bridge,
the military fully accoutred, and the cordons of police furnished a
centre-piece to a setting as peaceful as any artist could conceive. The
brackish waters of the Shannon, sparkling in the evening sunlight,
moved lazily by as if nothing was happening, and the
church bells intensified the calmness of the scene."
The Irish Times, 22 April 1919

The success and strength of the soviet may be gauged from the fact that only
four days after it began the authorities offered a tempting compromise.

On the first Thursday of the strike, Brigadier-General Griffin attended a
special meeting of the chamber of commerce, accompanied by his secretary,
Captain Wallace, County Inspector Crane from the RIC and District Inspector
Craig. [1] The proceedings were private, but a formal report was given to the press.
In order to facilitate the business of the city, General Griffin said, the authorities
had decided to allow the employers to issue permits to their employees. The
military would give the employers duplicate blocks of permits for this purpose.
Furthermore, at the request of the chairman and other members of the chamber,
he would put before headquarters the idea of granting a further concession so
that traders would be empowered to issue permits to their rural customers to
come in to shop in the city.

The general's meeting with the chamber may have been preceded by behind
the scenes contacts with major business people who were concerned about the
losses they would sustain in a continued strike. General Griffin's concession
represented a considerable climbdown on his part. At the start of the strike,
Cleeves had asked for a permit to cover all 600 of their workers, but this was
refused because the military had insisted on individual applications.

The General's offer was an ingenious device, firstly to divide what had
hitherto been a united community on the issue of permits, and secondly, to turn
the employers – who had at least acquiesced in the soviet's controls up to then
– into a pressure point on the workers to come to a settlement. It appears also

that the general was to some extent trying to use the employers as intermediaries to effect an overall solution to the problem. According to the *Workers' Bulletin*, General Griffin said that if the chamber saw fit they might consider conveying his decision to the strike committee. [2]

After General Griffin had left the chamber a strikers' delegation, led by John Cronin, was invited in and told of the offer. [3] The employers made it clear they hoped the offer would be accepted, emphasising too that they viewed it as a substantial concession. Cronin and his colleagues said they would report the matter to the full strike committee, but nothing further was heard on the matter, and it was, in practice, rejected out of hand.

In any event, the general's offer was unacceptable. Rank-and-file strikers interpreted the military compromise as giving the employers the right to decide who was fit to enter the city and who was not, something they could no more countenance than military checking. The danger was that some employers might abuse the power to discriminate against certain workers. Disappointed perhaps with this outcome, the chamber vented their irritation on the government and sent a resolution to Andrew Bonar Law, the acting prime minister, demanding that martial law be ended.

Easter Sunday, 20 April 1919, a week exactly after the strike began was, in some ways, a high point and a watershed of the Limerick soviet. Apart from its celebratory connotations in the Christian world, Easter in nationalist Ireland had an added significance. It is the time people commemorate the rising and executions of Easter 1916, seen as the modern spring from which the stream of freedom ran. Easter Sunday in Limerick became the occasion of a mass confrontation with the troops and police, that had many humorous aspects but was also a serious test by both sides of their will-power and resolution. One newspaper described the confrontation as "a situation of considerable menace" and another as "an ominous development". [4]

That Sunday evening, a crowd of about a thousand people, mostly young men and women, moved out of the city to the nearby Caherdavin Heights under the guise of attending a hurling or Gaelic football match. By this time, military permits were not needed to leave the city though they had been at the beginning of the strike. In any event, the military checkpoints were only on the main thoroughfares and it was always possible to leave the city along the railway bridges and embankments and by crossing the Shannon in a boat. Among the crowd were many of the strike leaders, including Tom Johnson, treasurer of the Trade Union Congress.

The Caherdavin episode is still shrouded in some mystery. Some survivors have asserted that no match was, in fact, planned and that, in reality, the exodus was nothing more than a ruse. The real aim, apparently, was to test the military's resolve.

After several hours, the large crowd moved back from the northern, Co. Clare, side of the Shannon, towards the sentries on Sarsfield Bridge. A soldier fired a blank shot and, immediately, military reinforcements rushed out of the Shannon Rowing Club and a dozen troops with loaded rifles and fixed bayonets moved to reinforce the sentries facing the crowd. In the upper windows of the clubhouse, troops placed guns in position. Officers rushed to and fro with their hands ominously on their revolvers and a nearby whippet tank on standby got up steam, tested its machine guns and moved into position.

For a time, it looked as if a serious crisis had been reached. The leaders of the crowd demanded entry to the city, without permits. This was refused. In an impressive display of passive resistance, the crowd then formed itself into a giant circle and, one by one, approached the sentries and demanded entry into Limerick, all the time just brushing off the bayonets. As each person was refused entry, they wheeled away and their place was taken by another.

Fifty policemen were marched down Sarsfield Street, from William Street Station, to reinforce the men on the bridge, but they carried only side arms and batons. A staff officer from military headquarters arrived on a motor-cycle, and a few minutes later, an armoured car – with machine guns ready for action – drove at a furious pace to the scene. News of the incident spread like wildfire through the city and thousands of people lined the city side of the river to watch the confrontation. A large number of journalists, including some American reporters, surveyed the scene.

Again and again, continuing until nightfall, the demonstrators marched in a circle right up to the military and police lines. The soldiers surveyed the parade in silence, but stood ready all the while with rifle and bayonet ready. Shortly after nine o'clock, the spectators scattered in panic as a rumour swept the crowd that the military were about to open fire. At one stage, a Franciscan priest crossed the bridge and appealed to the demonstrators, over the heads of the cordon, to disperse. General Griffin himself arrived to survey the problem at first hand.

The mayor, Alphonsus O'Mara, and a number of prominent citizens demanded that Griffin allow the demonstrators return to their homes. He offered to send an officer to give them permits, but this was refused and the mayor repeated his demand for unhindered passage, but without success.

The *Irish Times*, no friend of the strikers, carried this lyrical description of the demonstration: "The whole scene made a remarkable picture. The crowds on the bridge, the military fully accoutred, and the cordons of police furnished a centre-piece to a setting as peaceful as any artist could conceive. The brackish waters of the Shannon, sparkling in the evening sunlight, flowed lazily by as if nothing was happening, and the church bells intensified the calmness of the scene."[5]

From the city side of the river, there were shouts of encouragement and the

A military barricade on Thomond Bridge, with the Treaty Stone nearby.

demonstrators sang Irish songs to keep their spirits up. Shortly after midnight, a number of demonstrators managed to cross the river in boats. Despite the cold, others, including a large number of determined young women, maintained their vigil on the bridge. In the morning, some of the women passed unhindered through the military pickets. According to a local newspaper, the sentry's heart was softened by "their charming looks and the magic of their brogue". [6] Most of the demonstrators, however, spent the night in some comfort on the Clare side of the river. The women were accommodated in people's homes in the working-class Thomondgate district, famed in a local poem for "its social joys and the birthplace of the devil's boys". [7] The young men held an all-night concert and dance in St Munchin's Temperance Hall. Next morning, the Clare farmers brought hundreds of boxes of eggs, butter, gallons of new milk and loaves of homemade bread into Thomondgate. The residents cooked the food and the demonstrators all ate a hearty breakfast.

Fortified by their meal, after midday about 200 men and women lined up outside the Temperance Hall and marched about a mile to the Long Pavement railway station. They were cheered by crowds along the route. When they got to the station, they boarded a passenger train from Ennis, bound for Limerick. The station master and his staff were so astounded at this influx of passengers at a remote wayside station that they neglected to ask for tickets.

At the check platform outside the Limerick terminus, ticket checkers got on board and were amazed to find so many passengers without tickets. All of them paid their fare, however, without demurring. A number of military officers then arrived and demanded permits. When these were not forthcoming, they ordered the carriage doors to be locked and sentries placed outside. An attempt to segregate passengers who had permits, from the others, was abandoned as too laborious and time-consuming.

After a delay of half an hour, the train pulled in to the left-hand platform where double lines of sentries barred the way to the exits. A number of priests and nuns, who had permits, appealed in vain to be released from the carriages. All the while, the young passengers sang rebel songs.

Suddenly, all the carriage doors on the offside of the train from the military were opened, some of the young men having got keys, possibly from a friendly railway official. Between 200 and 300 men and women rushed out on to the centre platform and towards the main gate. Here armed sentries blocked the exit, but without pausing, the crowd rushed towards a side platform where only a solitary military policeman stood on guard. In vain, he held out his arms to block the rush. He was quickly brushed aside, and to the cheers of hundreds of onlookers gathered outside the station, the Caherdavin demonstrators broke the military blockade and were free.

The *Workers' Bulletin* revelled in the success of the demonstration. They described it as a highly successful entertainment put on by the soviet's "Amusement Committee" and watched by one of the largest audiences ever seen in Limerick. "The helmets shone, the rifles pealed, the police force performed acrobatic feats, the armoured cars ran wild, and even the auld tank – which apparently got more Scotch than soda – struck up *Rule Britannia* and sprawled out to greet the citizens of Limerick, and it was so delighted to meet them that it couldn't leave the way clear for them to get home." [8]

The British officers who boarded the train to check for permits were in remarkably good spirits and exchanged banter with the strikers. In general, there seems to have been a major difference in the strikers' attitude towards the military, compared to the Royal Irish Constabulary.

In the Easter Monday issue of the *Workers' Bulletin*, a writer expressed "the greatest feelings of joy that our fellow Trade Unionists in khaki are refusing to do the dirty work, which is only fit for such invertebrates as the RIC". [9] Occasionally, the *Bulletin* referred to the RIC as "swine", sometimes as the "Royal Irish Swine" or "Royal Irish Cowards". [10] On the other hand, the British soldiers were referred to as "Tommy", who was not the real enemy, merely "a tool of his Imperialistic, Capitalistic Government". [11]

There were few unpleasant incidents between the military and the civilian population. In some instances, the strike leaders with their distinctive badges were even saluted by the military. In general, the soldiers were considered to be carrying out their duties with tact and without unnecessarily interfering with people. Some of them became quite at home on the banks of the Shannon and "when freed from duty spend their time luring rebellious fish from its russet waters". [12]

As the strike continued, the soldiers began to tire of doing police work, and a major was court-martialled for refusing to do duties he considered proper to the constabulary. The *Workers' Bulletin* claimed an entire Scottish regiment was sent home for allowing people to go back and forth without passes. Obviously, so soon after the end of the Great War, the British army still contained many conscripts who held strong trade union or socialist views. As the *Bulletin* observed: "Men like to fight men on equal terms, but when it comes to dragooning one's own class, especially women and tender babes, in the interests of autocracy, it may become a different story." [13]

The attitude to the RIC was quite different. They were particularly resented as being "the eyes and ears" of British administration in Ireland. The RIC were a military force, armed with carbines and revolvers, and maintained at a strength of nearly 11,000 – well above that of a normal police force. The force had a peculiar legal status. It was not governed by the Army Act, but was an armed force governed by its own regulations. In this sense, it was unique in the British Empire. After the 1916 rising, the commander in chief in Ireland, General

Maxwell, had argued that the crisis had shown that he should have power to bring the constabulary under his direct orders in the event of another rebellion or an invasion and that, when so employed, they should be subject to military law. The RIC were native Irish men, but in order to minimise intimidation of their relatives they were not stationed in their home counties. There was hardly a village without an RIC barracks, in districts where ordinary crime was unknown. One of their principal tasks was to observe, and report on, anyone involved in any activity that threatened the state. That was wide enough to include Irish language and dancing classes and the Gaelic Athletic Association, the trade unions – especially the burgeoning Irish Transport and General Workers' Union – moderate nationalist groups like the Irish National Foresters, as well as Sinn Féin. Their reports were so comprehensive that a chief secretary for Ireland, Augustine Birrell, was able to boast to parliament: "We have the reports of the RIC who send us in, almost daily, reports from almost every district in Ireland, which enable us to form a correct general estimate of the feeling of the countryside in different localities." [14] An official report in 1919 said it was largely due to the efficiency of the RIC's excellent organisation that the 1916 rebellion had been kept within bounds and speedily suppressed throughout the country. [15]

The secessionist Dáil Eireann passed a decree of social ostracism against members of the RIC. This decree was enforced very effectively, forcing many policemen to resign and making it difficult to recruit replacements. Together with a large decrease in numbers to below its establishment figure, the decree ensured morale among the RIC was chronically poor during the Anglo-Irish War. It was partly for this reason that the authorities later turned to recruiting thousands of demobbed ex-servicemen and officers as members of the RIC. Because of the incongruous mix of khaki and bottle green in their early makeshift uniforms they were called the "Black and Tans" and later became notorious for their reprisals against the civilian population.

In Limerick, the circumstances of Robert Byrne's death – the jury's verdict blaming a policeman for the fatal wound – added to the bitterness with which the police were regarded. At the annual conference of the Drapers' Assistants' Association, held in Dublin during the period of the soviet, a Limerick delegate said "the military seemed to be friendly and the police were the only body who were not friendly". [16] In his speech to Robert Byrne's inquest, Patrick Lynch KC set the tone of Limerick's differing attitude to the military and police in the days that followed. [17] He asked how the semi-military police force had not turned their revolvers upon the attacking party of healthy men, but had killed the patient in the bed. The army, he said, were discharging what to them was a disagreeable and unpleasant task. He would say nothing that would make anyone think that those for whom he appeared entertained any feelings but one towards the military, because, by the instructions of the relatives of Robert Byrne, he would state publicly that they wished to express their appreciation of the courtesy and kindness extended to them in their trouble and sorrow by the military officers and men with whom they were brought into contact. When they left the city, they would leave it with the good wishes of every friend of Robert Byrne.

Lynch regretted to say he could not join in a similar expression of the manner in which the RIC force acted since the unfortunate tragedy. He could only attribute that to want of judgement. They lost their heads. Some of them acted in a manner that, he was sure, they, on cool reflection, would regret. Lynch's words were harsh, though in mitigation of the RIC's behaviour it might be argued that they had seen one of their own members shot dead in the workhouse incident, and another seriously wounded. The military, who had not suffered casualties, could perhaps therefore take a more benign view of events.

After a first week of triumphant success, the Limerick soviet was moving into its most testing period. Now the attitudes of the local employers, the Catholic bishop and clergy and the national trade union leadership became crucial to what would happen next.

CHAPTER TEN

Bosses and Clergy

"I wish to state that neither his Lordship nor the clergy were consulted
before the strike was declared, and they were teetotally opposed
to its continuance."
Rev. Fr W. Dwane, administrator, St Michael's parish,
reported in several newspapers

If the first week of the Limerick soviet had its moments of drama and comedy,
the second week turned into tragedy and, at times, farce. The main players in
determining the nature of this second act were the Catholic bishop, Dr Denis
Hallinan, the mayor, Alphonsus O'Mara, the military commander, General
Griffin, the leadership of the Irish Labour Party and Trade Union Congress, and
an assorted cast of strikers, employers and clergy.

The small shopkeepers and small businesses in general had co-operated with
the soviet from the beginning. But the major employers, represented by the
Chamber of Commerce, never did more than reluctantly acquiesce in the
workers' control of business life. Given the natural antagonism of interests
between the two classes this was not surprising. Almost from the start, the major
employers were champing at the bit. They met daily, testing ideas, probing
weaknesses, drafting formulae to allow the strike to be called off, liaising with
the British authorities, and in general, trying to restore what they saw as the
natural order of things in Limerick as quickly as possible.

On the first day of the strike, the Chamber of Commerce protested against the
proclamation of the city as a military area, particularly the irritating system of
permits, and they called for the immediate withdrawal of the restrictions. They
sent copies of their resolution to the lord lieutenant, Lord French, to General
Griffin and to the acting prime minister, Bonar Law. This may have prompted
the first concession by General Griffin, that of allowing the employers to issue
their own officially provided permits.

Only twenty-four hours after the strike started, prominent business people
were actively discussing the situation and complaining that their interests were
seriously affected. They suggested to the authorities that a slight alteration in the

mapping of the boundaries would overcome the difficulties that had provoked the strike – clearly underestimating the desire of the government to punish Limerick and the workers' revulsion at the prospect of having to obtain permits from any authority in order to go to work.

The Coal Merchants' Association publicly lost their patience with the strikers' controls more quickly than the other employers. On the first Wednesday of the strike, the Strike Committee ordered the coal merchants to open their yards. This was complied with and coal was sold to the citizens for a number of hours. But this type of workers' control was obviously too much for some of the coal merchants to swallow. The following day, Thursday, six of the principal merchants refused to open, and the police stood on duty outside their gates.

A deputation from the strike committee met the secretary of the Coal Merchants' Association and requested that the yards be re-opened. The merchants refused, saying they had no employees with which to do the necessary work. The deputation then offered to supply the necessary labour, but the secretary repeated that the yards would not be opened. There was little the strikers could do then – if a potentially violent confrontation was to be avoided – except to express considerable indignation at the merchants' attitude and point out that they had done everything possible to facilitate them, since the strike was called.

In contrast, the majority of provision merchants were reported to have acted in harmony with the strike committee and had kept prices at normal levels.

By the end of the first week, some employers were advocating a reopening of business premises on the Tuesday following the Easter weekend. They were prepared to carry on business as best they could, in defiance of the strike committee. John Cronin, chairman of the strike committee, warned they would oppose any such reopening, but without abusing the power in their hands. The proposal was discussed at a private meeting of the Chamber of Commerce, but the vast majority of opinion was against such a line of action. The chamber adjourned its meeting inconclusively.

A number of trade unions paid their members strike pay for the first week, and some employers decided to pay wages as well. T. Geary and Sons, the Shannon Confectionery Works, paid their staff full wages and Madge Daly paid the vandrivers of her dairy. Madge Daly was a member of a prominent Limerick Republican family. Her brother Edward, the only son and the youngest among a family of ten, was one of the commandants of the Easter week rebellion, in 1916, and had been executed by firing squad in the aftermath. Madge Daly and two of her sisters were leaders of Cumann na mBan, the Republican women's auxiliary group, and later during the Anglo-Irish War, their home was ransacked by the Black and Tans as part of official reprisals for an attack on British forces in Limerick.

Midway through the second week of the strike, the employers were still holding meetings and complaining about the strike's effect on their businesses. They saw themselves as the chief sufferers in a dispute to which they were not parties. They claimed many of their employees were anxious to return to work, but that the sinister spectre of the soviet stood in the way. Clerks in some offices returned to their desks, but they were immediately picketed. Some of the clerks stayed at work, but others rejoined the strikers.

One prominent employer made his representations directly to Bonar Law at No.10 Downing Street and to the lord lieutenant, Lord French. [1] He was George Clancy, a wholesale and retail draper. Clancy's suggestion was that the military restrictions be withdrawn or suspended, ostensibly temporarily, but that in reality the agitation that had caused the strike would then fizzle out. His clever argument was that since the citizens had behaved so peaceably during the strike, the authorities could claim they were lifting the restrictions as a reward for good behaviour. Now was the time to solve the problem, while it was easy to do so and no harm had been done. In his letter to Bonar Law he helpfully enclosed a copy of the *Irish Independent* to brief him on events in Limerick!

Clancy said that for many years prior to the strike, Limerick was perhaps "the quietest, most peaceful and most orderly place in the Empire". Describing the rescuers of Robert Byrne as "a party of foolish young fellows", he said the strike had been immediate and "down to the last man. The whole city was shut down. Factories, shops, business places of all kinds, large and small, solicitors' offices, Medical Halls. Everything shut down more rigorously than even on Sunday... Everything is exceptionally quiet, and most orderly so far."

But Clancy was worried the strike might lead to something more serious, and extend "over the whole of Ireland, North, South, East and West and it may be to England, Scotland and Wales, and I need not say what the result will be".

Clancy claimed he had made it his business to consult "a great many on both sides" – strike leaders and the heads of major firms like Cleeves. They were all quite unanimous that his idea was a splendid one. In his view, the "temporary" lifting of the restrictions would be "a great day's work for the Empire".

Clancy then cleverly couched his plea as one of concern for the prime minister, Lloyd George, who was in Paris "so terribly busy and his hands so very full finishing up in a highly satisfactory manner the mighty work of the Peace Conference". It would be cruel and inconsiderate on their part, Clancy wrote, to do anything that would cause the prime minister annoyance and worry and put more weight on his shoulders. On the contrary, they should try to make things "Easy and Pleasant" for him.

Clancy received no more than a routine acknowledgement of his letter from the acting prime minister at No.10.

Other prominent citizens were preoccupied too with the military controls on the city. On the first Saturday night of the strike, Holy Saturday, the mayor,

Alphonsus O'Mara, presided at a large meeting of citizens in the City Hall. [2]
They passed a resolution protesting against the imposition of the military area
system in Limerick. The resolution was proposed by Michael Collivet, the local
Sinn Féin MP (or TD as they were called in the separatist Dáil Eireann). Fr
O'Connor, parish priest of St. Mary's, proposed an addendum demanding the
instant withdrawal of the military cordon around the city since it prevented the
workers from having free access to their work.

John Cronin complained that coal and foodstuffs were being held up, and
another resolution was passed calling on people who had foodstuffs to place
them at the disposal of the people once they had got full market value for them.
Cronin's appeal is a significant measure of the weakness of the strikers' control
over fuel and food. The meeting also decided that the various bodies represented
should appoint delegates to a committee to help raise funds to alleviate distress.
Significantly, even at this relatively early stage, the Chamber of Commerce stood
aloof. Goodbody, vice-president of the chamber, said he and some other members were present, not to express any views, but to hold a sort of watching brief
and report to the chamber.

The mayor said that if the government was capable of governing they should
do so without punishing innocent people. If constitutional law existed in the
country, the city should not have been proclaimed. Michael Collivet called for
support for the strike committee, saying they had arrived at an acute stage of the
struggle. Collivet said that if a policeman had been killed or murdered in England
under the existing laws a military area such as had been enforced in Limerick
could not be maintained. If the people were beaten on that question it would
result in police law.

In his speech, John Cronin announced one of the most crucial developments
of the soviet – the impending arrival in the city of the entire executive council
of the Irish Labour Party and Trade Union Congress. On Monday and Tuesday,
Cronin predicted, "the seat of their Labour Parliament would be transferred from
Dublin to Limerick".[3] Indicating that he was thinking along the lines of a general
national strike as a result, Cronin said: "In the next day or two all Ireland would
be doing what Limerick was doing today."[4] Cronin declared that in calling the
strike they had done so with full responsibility, and were prepared to take the
consequences.

Tom Johnson, the congress treasurer, seemed to promise wider support too
when he said that Labour movements all over the world would respond to the
call of Limerick. "It was no longer a Limerick fight, but a fight of workers against
military domination and Imperialist forces."[5]

On the Saturday morning, the mayor had presided at a meeting of the city
magistrates. R.J. Daly proposed a resolution and it was seconded by the city
coroner, James F. Barry. It appealed, in the present grave crisis which had arisen,

to all lovers of peace and liberty to do all in their power to alleviate the deplorable conditions now prevailing, and declared that the military authorities would be well advised to extend the military area to such an extent that the citizens would be at liberty to attend their daily avocations without having to produce permits

There were two dissenting voices – O'Mara himself, and the resident magistrate, P.J. Kelly. [6] The mayor opposed the resolution on the formal grounds that the magistrates had not been consulted before the city was proclaimed, though probably his real objection was to the idea of extending the military boundaries further. The resident magistrate, on the other hand, rejected any implied criticism of the military arrangements.

The diligent Kelly recounted all this in a report to the under secretary for Ireland in Dublin Castle. [7] Mr Kelly apparently had the support of two others in opposing criticism of the military permits system. They were satisfied the military authorities had assessed all the facts before deciding on the boundaries of the proclaimed area. According to Kelly's report, "The majority of the Magistrates, with the Mayor, expressed themselves very strongly and pointedly showing that they are not at all in sympathy with the efforts of the authorities in the steps taken to maintain order. Some of them even went so far as to ignore the fact that a serious outrage took place at the Workhouse in the raid that was made and I'm sorry to say some conveyed that they thought it was the police who committed an outrage on that occasion."

Some allowance must be made for the fact that Kelly seems to have been particularly energetic in sniffing out sedition and promptly reporting it to senior officials in the Castle. Nevertheless, his comments give an illuminating insight into how far the attitudes of respectable and loyal citizens went in supporting the grievances that caused the strike.

By the time the Limerick Grand Jury convened for the summer assizes, in July, opinion of the RIC among the city's loyal and propertied classes had returned to more conventional lines. Sir Charles Barrington, Bart., proposed a resolution expressing most emphatically their admiration and high appreciation of the manner in which the members of the RIC had discharged their duty during the trying times through which they were now passing. [8] The Grand Jury tendered their warm sympathy to the relatives of those who had lost their lives, and they had much pleasure in sending a donation to the Central Benevolent Fund, RIC. The resolution was seconded by the Grand Jury foreman, J. O'G Delmege. The presiding judge, J. Samuels, directed that it be forwarded to the chief secretary for Ireland. On July 17 he replied fully endorsing the tribute paid by the Grand Jury to the members of the Royal Irish Constabulary and sharing their expression of sympathy with the relatives of those who had lost their lives.

But in any part of nationalist Ireland of the time the attitude of the Catholic bishop and clergy was crucial. Initially, the bishop, Dr Hallinan and the senior clergy came out strongly against the military proclamation and part of their statement was considered so strong in tone by the authorities that it was deleted by the censor.

The bishop met with clergy from the city parishes and the religious orders at St. Munchin's College on the third day of the strike. Afterwards, the newspapers published this statement:

[1] That we consider the proclaiming of the city of Limerick under existing circumstances as quite unwarrantable. Without explanation of any kind, the citizens of Limerick are being penalised for the lamentable events at the Limerick Workhouse.

[3] That in fixing the boundaries of the military area, the responsible authorities have shown a lamentable want of consideration for the citizens at large, and especially of the working classes.[9]

The censored portion included this strong criticism of the military surveillance of Robert Byrne's funeral:

[2] That the military arrangements of the funeral of the late Mr Robert Byrne were unnecessarily aggressive and provocative. The presence of armoured cars on the route and the hovering of aeroplanes over the city during the funeral procession were quite an uncalled for display, in the circumstances, of military power, and calculated to fill every right-minded person with feelings of disgust and abhorrence.[10]

This statement was signed by Denis Hallinan, bishop of Limerick, Canon David O'Driscoll, vicar general and parish priest of St. Munchin's, Canon David Keane, President St. Munchin's College, Fr Michael Murphy, parish priest of St. Patrick's, Fr O'Connor, parish priest of St. Mary's, Fr Connolly, administrator of St. John's Cathedral, Fr Bonaventure, guardian of the Franciscans, Fr Hennessy, prior of the Augustinians, Fr Fahy, prior of the Dominicans, the Jesuit rector, Fr Potter, Fr Dwane, administrator of St. Michael's and the Redemptorist Fr Kelly, director of the city's powerful Men's Arch Confraternity.

Not unexpectedly, there was no explicit approval for the strike, but the statement still indicated a degree of very significant and influential clerical support for a redressing of the grievances that had provoked the workers' action. With the bishop and the Catholic clergy apparently so firmly on their side, many strikers believed their success was assured. The *Irish Times* reported that the statement was generally regarded as a justification for the strike, and it had "infused fresh vigour into the members of the local soviet". [11]

This apparent clerical approval continued during the masses of the following

Sunday, Easter Day. In some Catholic churches, the priests congratulated the people on their good conduct, but appealed to juveniles not to congregate at street corners or jeer at the military sentries. This, apparently, was a practice that was increasingly irritating young soldiers. On Holy Saturday night, a sentry had fired a warning shot at some youths.

In the neighbouring Co. Clare diocese of Killaloe, we have already seen that Bishop Fogarty was an enthusiastic advocate of food supplies for Limerick. The efforts in this direction of Fr Kennedy of Ennis earned him the title of "A Fighting Soggarth" in one edition of the *Workers' Bulletin.* [12]

The attitude of the Limerick and Clare clergy may be contrasted with the remarks of the Catholic bishop of Ross, Dr Kelly, preaching in the Pro-Cathedral at Skibbereen, Co. Cork, a week after the workhouse shooting. [13] Dr Kelly said they knew there were deeds done in Ireland at present that were greatly against the doctrine of the Lord. They affected everyone, and were a blot on their country. He knew they were shocked at them, and he wanted them to do penance for them during Holy Week.

But the bishop was particularly concerned about expressions of approval for the soviet-led governments in Russia and Hungary that had been made that week during the sessions of Dáil Eireann. It was his duty as bishop to ask his flock to protest at those remarks, since the Russian and Austro-Hungarian revolutions were striking at the foundations of religion. The bishop said he had not been too concerned when Madame Markievicz – one of the Citizen Army leaders in the 1916 rebellion – had proclaimed support for the Russian Revolution, because he thought she stood alone. But now he was worried to read in his newspaper that these views were held by responsible members of parliament and some officials of the new "Government". As their bishop, he warned his congregation that if these ideas were spread among them, if they were picked up, "the faith of St. Patrick would not stand".

In its first edition of May, looking back at Limerick, the *Irish Catholic* carried an even more forthright condemnation under the heading "Irish Bolshevism". [14] The *Irish Catholic* first rejected the "crazy theories" that had "brought Russia to the verge of abyss". Then it turned to Limerick: "There is only one element of danger in the situation. That is the peril that arises from the possibility of the workers allowing themselves to be unconsciously misled. What has occurred in the city of Limerick is fresh in the public memory. As the result of certain manoeuvres, the import and true significance of which were certainly not manifest to the workmen when they struck, a crisis fraught with potentialities of grave trouble, not merely on a local, but on a national scale, was suddenly precipitated."

The *Catholic* continued: "The British sympathisers with Sovietism were naturally delighted at this development, but it is in accordance with the traditional tactics of these agitators that their social and industrial experiments should first be tried on the Irish dog. However, regarding the Limerick episode, it is one of those developments regarding which it can be said that all is well that ends well."

The editorial writer then trained his sights on Irish "agitators" who did not hesitate to invoke the example of Russian anarchism in furtherance of their political as well as their industrial propaganda. One of them had recently said Ireland had two chances: the first was President Wilson, the other was the Bolshevik rising in Russia. Rejecting what it called the "abominable evangel of Bolshevism", the newspaper said Lenin and his associates stood for relentless class warfare – the negation of democracy. Between those principles, and the principles of the faithful Catholic people of Ireland there could be no compromise.

With attitudes like these so prevalent among influential Catholic leaders of the time, it was inevitable that the uneasy coalition of interests opposing the military proclamation would come under strain, and then crumble. The catalyst for this development was the arrival in Limerick, in the second week of the soviet, of the executive of the Irish Labour Party and Trade Union Congress.

CHAPTER ELEVEN

The Workers Defeated

"The struggle would have dragged on for some time longer had not his
Lordship, Most Rev. Dr Hallinan, and the Mayor, as representing the
spiritual and temporal interests of the citizens sent a joint letter
to the Trades Council on Thursday requesting the
immediate end of the strike ... "
The Munster News, editorial entitled
"The Strike–And After" (26.4.1919)

The first notification the executive of the Irish Labour Party and Trade Union
Congress had of the Limerick situation was a telegram sent by John Cronin, and
received by William O'Brien, general secretary of the congress, on the first day
of the strike, Monday, 14 April 1919. The telegram read: "General strike here
as protest against military restrictions." [1] O'Brien replied by telegram wishing
the strikers success and asking to be kept informed of events. The general
secretary got no reply and rang up the newspaper offices looking for information.
He got what information appeared in the evening papers.

Communications were obviously not easy and some union leaders in Dublin
suspected the authorities were intercepting messages from Limerick, and consequently, information was hard to come by.

On Tuesday there was still no information from Limerick, so the following
day, O'Brien called together all the available members of the executive and they
discussed the matter informally. In the absence of information, they decided the
best thing to do was to send someone to Limerick, and that job was given to
Thomas Johnson, the congress treasurer.

Johnson was born in Liverpool in 1872 and served from 1914 to 1916 as
president of the Trade Union congress, having attended his first congress in 1911,
as a delegate of the National Union of Shop Assistants and Clerks. From 1903
onwards, he had worked in Belfast for a cattle food firm until dismissed from
his job as a commercial traveller because of his public opposition to conscription,
but his attitude to Republicanism was cautious. In 1918, he was appointed
full-time treasurer of the congress. Johnson was a little old-fashioned in his trade

unionism, neither Marxist nor nationalist. Yet he showed a remarkable sensitivity to the complexity of Irish society and had the capacity to understand North and South, both Belfast and Dublin.

The great leaders of Irish trade unionism of the early decades of this century, Connolly and Larkin, as well as Johnson, were born in Britain. But in many ways, Johnson typified British trade unionism much more than the other two.

Johnson got a permit from the authorities and arrived in Limerick on the third day of the strike. He was a hardworking organiser and a thoughtful public speaker, and he seems to have established an immediate rapport with the strike leaders. He was one of the most prominent people involved in the Caherdavin incident, and the *Workers' Bulletin* of 23 April paid him this tribute: "To the splendid efforts of Tom Johnson, the defence of Limerick owes much, and his intrepid bravery has won him many friends in Limerick and elsewhere." [2]

Back in Dublin, two Limerick railway men arrived to look for support for the strike. They met their colleagues of the National Union of Railwaymen (NUR) at the Inchicore Engineering works, a pivotal part of the network of the Great Southern and Western Railways. The response was lukewarm.

The Dublin NUR men said that unless there was an extension of the strike to places like Cork and Tralee, Dublin would remain uninvolved. A spokesman for one of the biggest NUR branches in Dublin told the *Irish Independent* that while he sympathised with the Limerick people, he thought the policy adopted was a mistaken one. [3] It did not inconvenience the military, who had ample means of transporting their supplies, but it meant starvation for their own people. They in Dublin had painful recollections of a somewhat similar state of things during their 1916 strike.

The two NUR men briefed congress executive members on the position in Limerick as it stood at their departure. The executive also met a delegation from the Railway Workers' emergency committee, a national co-ordinating body representing the major rail unions. The emergency committee pointed out that if the Limerick men stopped work, the whole Great Southern railway system would be "put out of gear". [4] The railway men made it clear they were prepared to come out on strike, but only with other workers as part of a national strike.

That same day, William O'Brien and other TUC leaders began a series of meetings spread over three days with the executive, or government, elected by the separatist parliament, Dáil Eireann. The aim, presumably, was to see to what extent the two bodies could, or should, co-ordinate their action over Limerick. Not unexpectedly, the Dáil executive does not seem to have encouraged more widespread trade union action. They may have had practical objections to such action, but equally likely, Sinn Féin may not have liked the prospect of effectively handing over leadership of the militant part of the independence struggle so clearly to the trade unions. For a variety of reasons, many of the Dáil executive

Limerick rail engineering works, a major focal point of the soviet. Strike-bound engineering facilities here did not prevent trains from running because other rail workers continued to operate them.

would have wanted to maintain control, and the premier position, for themselves.

The congress leaders began to realise that any further escalation of support for Limerick would be entirely on their own heads and would lack the enthusiastic national support of Sinn Féin. They had to look for an alternative that would save face all round. At some stage over the three days of meetings with the Dáil representatives, Tom Johnson and William MacPartlin came up with the idea of a peaceful evacuation of the entire city. By doing this, the aim was to focus worldwide attention on the plight of the workers in Limerick, without the prospect of bloodshed.

The available resident members of the executive met and discussed the idea, and O'Brien summoned the non-resident members by telegram to a meeting the following day, Holy Thursday. The full executive agreed on the evacuation plan of action and arranged to meet in Limerick after the Easter weekend. In the meantime, O'Brien and the vice-president, Thomas Farren of the ITGWU, who was also secretary of the influential Dublin trades council, were to join Tom Johnson in Limerick immediately. O'Brien, in fact, never travelled to Limerick and this later became a focus of friction between local trade unionists and the national leadership.

Outwardly, the National Executive seemed determined in its support for the Limerick strike. It unanimously condemned the action of the military authorities in proclaiming a military area in Limerick, in preventing the free movement of the Limerick trade unionists to and from their work, and in depriving them of their rights as workers and citizens. In a statement, it called for the immediate abrogation of the order making permits to work obligatory in Limerick. The statement went on: "In view of this wanton attack on trade unionists, the National Executive appeals to the unbiased opinion of the workers and peoples of all countries as to on whose shoulders lies responsibility for the probably grave consequences which this unwarrantable and unnecessary action by the military may precipitate."[5]

The following day, in Limerick, before any of his colleagues had arrived, Tom Johnson seemed to commit them to a national stoppage in support of Limerick. In a statement to the press, he interpreted the executive's resolution as an endorsement of, and full support for, Limerick. Johnson said he had authority to announce that the full strength of the Labour movement in Ireland, backed by the general public, would be exerted on behalf of the men and women of Limerick. The national executive, in collaboration with the strike committee, would take such action as would ensure victory. "This is," Johnson declared, "in the first instance, Labour's fight against the attempt by the British military authorities to choose who shall, or shall not, proceed to or from his or her daily work, but it is also Limerick's reply to President Wilson's question, 'Shall the military power of any nation or group of nations, be suffered to determine the fortunes of peoples over whom they have no right to rule, except the right of force?' Limerick's reply is 'No', and all Ireland is at her back." [6]

Johnson said the national executive were determined to give the strike committee all possible support. They realised that while it was Limerick today, tomorrow it might be other great cities like Cork, Waterford, Dublin, Derry or Belfast. The national executive, he said, congratulated the committee and workers on the splendid way they had upheld the banner of liberty. It would show that the men and women of 1919 were no less valiant than those of 1690, the year of the first Williamite siege of Limerick.

The Limerick strikers could be forgiven for thinking the full weight of the Irish trade union movement was about to be thrown behind them in a national strike. But it was not to be.

Firstly, there appeared to be difficulties about a speedy transfer of the full executive to Limerick. No trains were running on Good Friday, but four members of the executive made it to the city on Easter Tuesday. They were Thomas Farren of the ITGWU, vice-president of congress, John T. O'Farrell of the Irish Railway Clerks' Association, Rose Timmons and T.C. Daly, a member of the National Union of Railwaymen. Thomas Farren had taken part in the 1916 rising and was one of a group of trade union leaders with nationalist sympathies who were arrested afterwards. O'Farrell, in the 1922 general election, missed a seat in the Irish Free State Dáil by only thirteen votes but was elected to the Senate. The general secretary, William O'Brien, remained in Dublin. Another visitor to Limerick that day was the general officer commanding-in-chief for Ireland, Sir Frederick Shaw, who conferred with General Griffin, the commandant, military area.

Matters cannot have been helped by the involvement of the congress president, Thomas Cassidy, in organising the Easter conference of his union. His association's general president had come over from Britain to assist him and was, in fact, the first person to tell Cassidy about the Limerick strike. Apparently, Cassidy and his president were travelling around the country on union business. That prevented him going to Dublin for the full executive meeting summoned by O'Brien. Instead, on Easter Monday and Tuesday his association's executive ordered him to Drogheda, Co. Louth, on union business. Cassidy considered, rightly or wrongly it is difficult to judge, that his own union's affairs should take precedence over consideration of Limerick.

William O'Brien felt it was better to wait to have the full executive available to take decisions on what was a very serious issue. Consequently, Easter Tuesday, eight days after the strike had started, was the first day on which members of the executive could travel to Limerick. In fact, they did not arrive in the city until the Wednesday, the ninth day of the strike, when they went into a long session of talks with the strike committee. The *Irish Times* – with hindsight, it seems correctly – interpreted the failure to meet the Tuesday appointment as "an indication that all is not not well in official Labour circles". [7]

From the moment they arrived in Limerick that Wednesday, the full congress leadership were in almost continuous meetings with the strike committee discussing strategy and tactics. At their first long meeting, chaired by John Cronin, the congress delegation consisted of: Thomas Farren, the vice-president; T.C. Daly, National Union of Railwaymen; John T. O'Farrell, Irish Railway Clerks' Association; Michael O'Lehane, Drapers' Assistants; Councillor Michael J. Egan, a coachmaker from Cork; Tom Johnson, the congress treasurer; and Rose Timmons. O'Lehane was a staunch member of Sinn Féin. Egan was one of three congress delegates, along with senior figures like O'Brien and Johnson on the nine man "national cabinet" put forward by the Mansion House conference to oppose conscription in 1918. The RIC duly reported to Dublin Castle on a strikers' meeting held on this date. [8]

Officially, the congress leaders claimed they were there to assist the strike committee, not to take charge of the dispute. But differences of opinion emerged even on that first day. Understandably, in the light of the earlier statements by the executive and Johnson, John Cronin and the other strike leaders wanted the congress to declare a national strike in support of Limerick. Some of the congress leaders claimed their constitution did not give them the power to do that – the calling of strikes, local or national, was a matter for the individual union affiliates.

The congress leaders' opposition to a national strike, however, was much more fundamental than any constitutional niceties. They recognised the potential for Limerick to escalate into a bloody revolutionary conflict with Britain if it was pushed to a national strike. The congress had neither the physical means nor had it developed the political consciousness among its rank-and-file members to pursue or defend such a strategy. From their meetings in Dublin, they already knew they could not count on the wholehearted support of Sinn Féin, the IRA or the Dáil. There were doubts over whether the National Union of Railwaymen could be relied on to paralyse transport in such a strike, and without doubt, the Unionist workforces of Ulster would actively oppose it. There was uncertainty too over how trade unionists and socialists in Britain would react to such a development in Ireland.

People like Tom Johnson might accept that Limerick was justified in calling for a national strike, but the real question was whether it was the correct strategy, knowing it would have resulted in armed revolt. Johnson believed that some day an insurrection might be developed out of Labour agitation, but it should not be because of Limerick.

The congress leaders advanced the alternative plan they had already hatched before leaving Dublin: the complete evacuation of the city by its inhabitants, leaving it an empty shell in the hands of the military. The executive leaders stressed that they did not propose this in any haphazard way, but had made undisclosed arrangements to house and feed the people of Limerick if they agreed to the plan. The merit they saw in their proposal was that it did not involve the prospect of any blood being shed, and it would make for very effective propaganda in Britain, Europe and the United States.

Not surprisingly, perhaps, the strike leaders flatly rejected the proposal. Whatever chance there was of feeding and housing people in their own city, with the benefit of outside help, they could have little faith in the ability of the Irish Labour Party and Trade Union Congress to feed and house about 40,000 men, women and children outside Limerick. In addition, property owners and professional people like doctors, solicitors or dentists, many of whom were sullen and reluctant inhabitants of Limerick under the soviet, were not likely to abandon the city on the recommendation of a trade union body.

Apart from the Dáil's attitude, the railwaymen were central to the executive's dilemma. The railways were the main method of mass transport of people and goods over long distances, and therefore were of crucial strategic and economic importance. Johnson's assessment that the military would not stand idly by and let the railways be paralysed was almost certainly correct.

The Limerick railway workers had served strike notice which was due to expire at midnight on 16 April, the first Wednesday of the general strike. But, even as Tom Johnson was setting off for Limerick, his colleague William O'Brien was telegraphing the rail workers saying: "Railwaymen should defer stoppage pending national action. National Executive specially summoned for tomorrow." [9] This was sent after the TUC had consulted the rail delegates from Limerick, the Dublin rail workers at Inchicore, the Railwaymen's Emergency Committee, as well as the national Republican leadership. That telegram had been the first real indication that whatever ways the Limerick strike might develop, they did not include a national strike.

Some rail employees in Limerick had already gone on strike on Tuesday, 15 April. These were members of the Amalgamated Society of Engineers, employed in the smith, machine and fitting shops. They were followed the next day by the boiler-makers, but the stoppage of those categories in no way interfered with the running of the trains. The leaders of the Limerick strike remained optimistic that their strike would spread to the other parts of the province of Munster served by the Great Southern and Western Railway. Towards the end of their first week, John Cronin said delegates who had visited various centres had returned to Limerick with reports that other workers were unanimous in their support for Limerick. He said the railway workers in other districts were ready to go out "when the call was made". [10]

But despite those early indications of some trade union help elsewhere in

The failure of the National Union of Railwaymen in particular to support the Limerick soviet was a major factor in its defeat. Some Limerick rail engineering workers joined the strike, but could not prevent the trains running. The Limerick rail engineering workers above were employed by the Great Southern and Western railway.

Ireland, the attitude of the British unions with members in Ireland and especially the National Union of Railwaymen, remained crucial. As the *Daily Herald* put it: "The success or failure of the strike is dependent on the railwaymen's action."

The British trade union answer was clear and sharp. The general secretary of the National Union of Railwaymen, Jimmy Thomas MP, sent a circular directing their Irish branches to advise their members that: "they must not take any official part in what appears to be an industrial move against political action, without the authority from the Executive Committee". [11] On Thomas's instructions, a copy of his circular was sent to the Limerick branch of the NUR and to all railway branches in Ireland. The circular followed a report on Limerick and a discussion at the national executive of the NUR.

For the British Trade Union Congress, H.R. Stockman issued a statement to the press. The executives of the British trade unions concerned held that their Irish branches could not be allowed to strike in Ireland, because they were opposed to the use of trade union machinery for political ends. Significantly, officials were advised that their members in Belfast were "almost entirely opposed to a strike". [12] This was a point noted too by the *Irish Times* in its editorial on the morning when the rest of the executive arrived in Limerick. [13]

Irish emigrants were not without influence in the British trade unions. There was speculation that if an unauthorised stoppage went ahead in Ireland, there would be sympathetic strikes of railmen and other workers in areas where there were large Irish communities. The same was said about the general transport workers, particularly in Liverpool and other towns with large Irish populations. Stockman himself admitted that there was a very strong agitation among the rank-and-file of the railwaymen "on the English side of the Channel" in favour of sympathetic action in support of the Irish strikers.

In August 1919 as the Anglo-Irish war intensified, Tom Johnson, as secretary of the Irish Labour Party and Trade Union Congress, reported that Irish workers on Tyneside and Clydeside wanted to organise and be affiliated to the Irish congress. In April 1920 Irish workers in Liverpool and Hull struck in sympathy with Sinn Féin prisoners in Wormwood Scrubs Prison.

The leaders of the British trade unions were not without sympathy for the Limerick workers in their difficulties, but they insisted that any action should be in accordance with their union rule books. It was decided to ask the Labour Party to raise the issue in parliament without delay and to enlist the support of Liberal and other MPs for a demand that the government deal with the Irish question on lines likely to remove the necessity for maintaining martial law in Limerick or anywhere else.

The local newspaper, the *Munster News*, took the view that Stockman's statement very probably marked the turning point of the dispute. [14] It seemed to this newspaper that while Irish trade unions were frequently called upon to support strikes in Britain, reciprocity could not be counted on. Without the support of the British trade union executives, the Irish Labour Party and Trade Union Congress probably had little option but to rule out a national strike. But it was their "extreme" proposal of the peaceful evacuation of Limerick that prompted, and allowed, the Catholic bishop to intervene in the strike and set in motion the events that led to its eventual end. On Thursday, 24 April, the bishop, Dr Hallinan, and the mayor, Alphonsus O'Mara, began what would be termed in modern parlance a round of "shuttle diplomacy". The *Irish Independent* described it as "an anxious day of conferences and 'conversations'". [15]

It was the national executive's second day in Limerick, and in the morning the bishop and the mayor met the strikers and the national union leaders. That meeting was adjourned, while the two public figures went to a lengthy meeting with General Griffin. Griffin repeated his earlier offer, made to the employers and traders, of allowing them to issue permits themselves to their workers and customers. And he offered a further major concession. To lighten the restrictions on workers, he would agree not to check passes when they were going to or from their meals. These combined concessions were enough to change the minds of the bishop and the mayor.

When the combined strike/congress committee resumed their deliberations in the afternoon, they had before them a joint letter from the bishop and the mayor. They urged the leaders to end the strike. Further light is thrown on the contents of the letter by an editorial headed "The Strike – And After" in the *Munster News*: "The struggle would have dragged on for some time longer had not his Lordship, Most Rev Dr Hallinan and the Mayor, as representing the spiritual and temporal interests of the citizens, sent a joint letter to the Trades Council on Thursday, requesting the immediate end of the strike ... " [16] A search of the Limerick Catholic diocesan records failed to locate a copy of the letter, so its contents must be inferred from contemporary reports and comments. With the Catholic Church, the Chamber of Commerce and even some merchants with Sinn Féin sympathies now ranged against the strike, and with the Trade Union Congress more a hindrance than a help, the strikers had run out of options.

The *Irish Times* had no doubt that the change of attitude on the part of the Catholic Church was decisive. The Church's earlier position of support was not maintained. "It is freely stated here that their views of the situation completely changed when they learnt of the drastic plans submitted by the Labour Executive to force the issue. They naturally discountenanced extreme measures and the Executive, knowing that the people would be guided by their clergy, wisely abandoned their plans." [17]

As night drew in and word spread that momentous matters were being discussed, several thousand people gathered outside the Mechanics' Institute. John Cronin appeared at a window and congratulated the people on their magnificent stand against tyranny. He said the fight would go on, and the flag would be kept flying.

But it fell to Tom Johnson to make a dramatic announcement to the press. [18] The strike committee called on all workers who could resume work without having to apply for permits to do so the following morning. Other workers who still needed permits would remain on strike, but there would be a national congress of the Irish Labour Party and Trade Union Congress to consider further action. The effect of this decision was to allow the majority of strikers to resume work, but the 600 employees of Cleeves were still affected, as were a considerable number of workers in the Thomondgate district.

From subsequent discussions at the Trade Union Congress it is clear that the proposal to hold a special conference was never intended as a serious proposition. It was intended more to ease the psychological blow of capitulation for the strikers and to maintain a semblance of continuing pressure against the permits system.

Councillor Robert O'Connor, a member of the strike committee, read the proclamation which was to be posted up on the streets: "Whereas the workers of Limerick have been on strike since Monday, 14 April, as a protest against the military ban on our city; and whereas, in the meantime the question has become a national issue, we hereby call upon all workers who can resume work without permits to do so on tomorrow (Friday) morning. We further call upon all those workers whose daily occupation requires them to procure military permits to continue in their refusal to accept this sign of subjugation and slavery, pending a decision of the Irish Trade Union Congress, to be called immediately. We also call upon all our fellow-countrymen and lovers of freedom all over the world to provide the necessary funds to enable us to continue this struggle against military tyranny. Strike Committee, 24 April 1919." [19]

The announcement was received with mixed feelings, and in silence, by the assembled strikers. Many were glad to be returning to work, though others regarded the result as a defeat and felt their sacrifices had gone for nothing. The *Irish Times*, strangely, reported that Johnson was received with cheers, but the *Independent* said the speeches of their leaders did not put the strikers in better heart. [20]

In his speech, Johnson said that, taking everything into account, they had taken the best course for the moment. They believed the fight had been taken up by the workers of Limerick on behalf of the people of Ireland as a whole. It was the duty of Ireland to continue it, and if Ireland was going to let the workers of Limerick down, Ireland must be ashamed of herself and need no longer call herself a fighter for freedom. He complimented the workers on the way they had governed the city so well – as good as any government.

The crowds dispersed quietly and during the evening copies of the proclama-

PROCLAMATION

WHEREAS the Workers of Limerick have been on Strike since Monday, 14th April, as a protest against the Military Ban on our City, and

WHEREAS, in the meantime the question has become a National issue, we hereby call upon all workers who can resume work without Military Permit to do so on

TO-MORROW
(FRIDAY MORNING)

WE further call upon all those workers whose daily occupation requires them to procure Military Permits to

CONTINUE
IN THEIR REFUSAL

to accept this sign of subjugation and slavery, pending the decision of a special Irish Trade Union Congress to be called immediately.

WE also call upon our fellow-countrymen, and lovers of Freedom all over the World to provide the necessary funds to enable us to continue this struggle against Military Tyranny.

STRIKE COMMITTEE

Limerick April 24th. 1919.

This proclamation, on 24 April 1919, was the first public recognition by the soviet of its impending defeat. It allowed a resumption of work by strikers who did not need military permits to get to their jobs, while a minority of workers remained on strike. But, solidarity had crumbled.

tion were posted throughout the city. Some members of the ITGWU were far from happy. They tore up the posters and burned them in disgust. Some of them threatened to set up another soviet, but these threats were probably not intended to be taken seriously. The feeling of resentment against the strike leaders was short-lived.

The following day, Friday, there was a hurried attempt to resume business, but it was mainly confined to a small section of traders. For some factories, there was a shortage of raw materials, and in others where furnaces had to be stoked up, there was not enough time overnight to prepare them for re-opening. In the case of the bacon factories, they had no pigs to slaughter since fairs and buying had been suspended.

For General Griffin, the decision in favour of a return to work by a large number of strikers was a triumph for the careful and shrewd way he had handled the strike. His background as a member of a Catholic family from Cork may have been a help. General Griffin applied the military regulations with a firm, but light, hand. He was anxious, no doubt, to avoid any provocative action or confrontation that might spark off an escalation of the strike.

In contrast to the days preceding Robert Byrne's burial, there was not a high level of military or police activity in the city under the military regulations. Most troops and police were confined to barracks and the emphasis was on manning checkpoints on the boundaries of the military area. Even that was done in a low-key way. Only the bridges facing north across the Shannon were fully manned. After some days, no one was prevented from leaving the city without a permit and it was easy enough to cross the river by boat. On the south side of the city – where it met Co. Limerick – access was uninhibited.

No one was actually charged with illegal entry and on only two occasions did soldiers shoot to prevent entry. On neither occasion was anyone caught, though on one of them, it was claimed a donkey was shot and became the first victim of the siege! Nevertheless, Griffin's position was strengthened by the resolute way the military had seen off the challenge of the Caherdavin demonstrators on Easter Monday.

General Griffin was hampered by not being able to use any of the city's printing works to produce counter-propaganda. On the first evening of the strike, his soldiers posted a typewritten notice blaming the strikers for any hardship caused. But that was the only feeble attempt to counteract the strikers' very active propaganda committee.

The general was shrewd enough not to try to break the strike by military intervention. That might have provided further martyrs and justification for stronger action on the other side. He did not try to prevent the pickets from closing down businesses. Instead, Griffin chose to wait for the realisation to dawn that the strike either had to escalate or be ended. In this, he proved ultimately to have a number of unlikely and unexpected allies in the national and local leadership of Sinn Féin, the Catholic bishop and clergy, the mayor and the leadership of the Irish Labour Party and Trade Union Congress. Griffin's "wait and see" strategy relied on splitting the city's solidarity by offering tempting concessions to the employers, who were at best, reluctant parties to the dispute at any time. The initial strength of the strikers, and the early support of Sinn Féin people like O'Mara and Collivet, the Sinn Féin TD, was enough to stave off the employers' revolt. But once it became clear, in the second week of the strike, that the ILPTUC was not going to support a national strike, the general had only to restate his earlier concessions for them to be accepted with alacrity. In achieving an end to the strike, the general maintained the government's status and the army's morale, by dealing only with the employers, the mayor and the bishop. In that way, he denied any recognition to the strike leaders, something the employers probably welcomed because of its long term beneficial side effects for them.

On 26 April, the Saturday after the partial return to work, a statement from Johnson made it clear there had been a clash over strategy and tactics between the local leaders and the national leadership. [21] The executive had submitted "certain proposals of a drastic character" which they believed would be the most effective way of countering the military tyranny using peaceful means. To their regret, the strike committee had told them their proposals were not likely to receive the necessary support and they accepted that decision as final. Curiously, the *Irish Times* report says the executive "endorsed" the local decision. [22] It is not quite clear from the statement whether the strike committee had turned down the "drastic" evacuation proposal on its merits, or whether they were influenced by the bishop's opposition.

Johnson made the, by then, almost ritualistic comments congratulating the workers on their administrative and organisational abilities, and called for financial assistance to meet the losses already incurred and to continue the fight. The national executive asked that any money be sent to James Casey, the trades council treasurer, at the Mechanics' Institute in Limerick. With that final statement, all the members of the congress executive, except Johnson, left Limerick.

The conduct of the strike was now back in the hands of the local strike committee. The various sub-committees remained at work, and concentrated on helping people who needed money or food.

For a time, the question of employers issuing permits to their employees flared as an issue. This was one thing on which the strike committee and the congress executive could agree on even at the height of their disagreements – no worker could accept a permit to work from the hands of their employer. Some workers who took these permits were, on that final Saturday, stopped by pickets and ordered back, while some carters refused employers' permits given to them to make deliveries outside the city. The Thomondgate people seemed determined to continue a protest and they held a general meeting of some of the residents on the Friday night. On Saturday morning a number of them blocked Thomond Bridge and deterred some people from crossing. The police were called and dispersed what seems to have been a halfhearted attempt at a blockade.

Other workers resorted to ingenious devices to return to work without having to request permits. A few procured tents to camp outside the military boundaries and others went to live temporarily in the areas where they were employed. Late on Sunday night, 27 April, the strike committee issued another proclamation: "Whereas for the past fortnight the workers of Limerick have entered an emphatic and dignified protest against military tyranny, and have loyally obeyed the orders of the Strike Committee, we, at a special meeting assembled, after carefully considering the circumstances, have decided to call upon the workers to resume work on Monday morning. We take this opportunity of returning our thanks to every class of the community for the help tendered during the period of the strike." [23] The Limerick soviet had ended as suddenly as it began exactly fourteen days previously.

John Cronin sent a telegram to the congress executive in Dublin announcing the end of the strike and stating that the strikers had decided that the holding of a special trade union congress should be abandoned.

CHAPTER TWELVE

Green, Red and Orange

"They were all anxious for unity, and no threat of cleavage had been
made if the motion brought forward by the Limerick delegates failed.
Unity was very good, but if it came to a question of principle,
then let them scrap unity."
Tipperary Delegate, Mr Mansfield, to the Irish National Teachers'
Organisation annual congress, Good Friday, 25 April 1919

The Catholic clergy and the employers were quick to recriminate against the
strikers. On the final Sunday of the strike – the day the full resumption of work
was decided on – Fr Dwane, administrator of St. Michael's parish strongly
criticised the conduct of the strike. [1] Addressing the congregation at twelve
o'clock mass, he said neither the bishop nor the clergy were consulted before
the strike was declared, and they were totally opposed to its continuance.

Fr Dwane said his sympathies were always with the working classes. He was
a great believer in the dignity of labour, and any help he could give in raising
the dignity of labour would be rendered by him on all occasions. But he had a
stern warning for his listeners: "He hoped the honest working men of Limerick
would in future duly consider any action they were about to take, and be guided
only by leaders upon whom they could rely and in whom they could have full
confidence, and not allow themselves to be fooled or deceived by anybody
whatsoever. He was very glad the strike had ended, and it was highly creditable
that during its continuance everything was so peaceable and orderly in the city."

The employers were piqued because they were not told officially of the
strike's partial end on the Thursday. The Chamber of Commerce at that stage
decided on a phased re-opening of business beginning with shops and flour mills,
and leaving the factories until after the weekend.

In a later statement, however, they made what they termed an emphatic protest
against the calling of a general strike without giving due notice to the employers.[2]
Had the positions been reversed, and the employers had closed their premises
without notice, they believed the workers would have bitterly resented the action.
The Chamber of Commerce argued that if the workers had consulted with them

before calling the strike, they might have been able to take joint action that would have saved the city from a "disastrous" strike. As it was, the chamber estimated the employers had lost about a quarter of a million pounds in turnover and that the workers had lost £42,000 in wages.

The disdainful attitude of the employers and other prominent citizens towards the strike was underlined some days after the permit system was withdrawn when a delegation of Irish-American politicians visited Limerick. This stop-over was part of a fact-finding tour of Ireland to observe the situation at first hand. At no time during the welcoming speeches of the mayor or high sheriff were the strike or the military occupation mentioned. None of the visitors referred to it either, an indication perhaps that it was regarded as an aberration and not part of the true nationalist tradition.

Whatever about local criticism or opposition from employers or clergy, the Limerick soviet attracted widespread interest and some support from outside the city during its existence. This support came, not unexpectedly, from trade union and labour organisations, but also from public bodies and the Gaelic Athletic Association, and it came from Britain as well as other parts of Ireland.

One of the first outside bodies to protest against the military restrictions was Waterford trades council.[3] On the day the strike began, they passed a resolution demanding the immediate withdrawal of military law from all the areas affected. A copy of the resolution was forwarded to MacPherson, the chief secretary for Ireland. Other trades councils sent messages of support, money and other practical help to Limerick. Galway trades council planned to organise a May Day concert for Limerick. Cork trades council set up a fund and protested against the "military dictatorship established by the army of occupation". Cork Grocers' and Allied Trades' Assistants had called for the setting up of such a fund and the gas workers there promised support. Tralee trades council collected forty pounds for the strikers.

Other trades councils, faced with local strikes of their own, found it difficult to raise money for Limerick, so there was little question of the councils banding together outside the control of the Irish TUC to produce sympathetic action. Wexford trades council expressed regret that because of a local foundry dispute they could not help. Similar problems arose in Dundalk, Drogheda, Boyle and other areas. In neighbouring Co. Clare, however, Ennis trades council assured Limerick of their unqualified support in whatever the Irish TUC deemed necessary to secure victory.

The national executive of the Irish Transport and General Workers' Union voted the considerable sum of £1,000 towards the strike. As a first instalment, the national executive of the Irish Clerical Workers' Union sent £100 to the strike committee. There was further clerical workers' support from the Dublin branches of that union. Another national executive that voted a hundred pounds was the Irish Automobile Drivers' Union. A double levy of four pence was made on workers in Athlone, Co. Westmeath, and in the same county, Mullingar branch of the ITGWU opened a subscription list and passed a resolution condemning the action of the authorities in Limerick. From Derry came a pledge of support from the city's dockers and carters for Limerick in the "fight against militarism".

The annual conference of the Drapers' Assistants' Association, representing £5,000 shop assistants and clerks, unanimously condemned the action of the government or military authorities in their treatment of the workers of Limerick in preventing them from freely earning their daily bread, and they pledged them their strongest support in the struggle for freedom.

Two Limerick delegates, in their speeches, gave interesting insights into conditions there. Mr Daly said the military seemed to be friendly and the police were not. He said the strike committee's control was so complete that even Major Wood had to apply for a permit before he could attempt his flight to America, and he had acknowledged that he did so with the committee's permission. Mr Connaughton, also from Limerick, referred to the anomalies in the way the military had mapped the boundaries. In St. Patrick's parish, he said, the barrier came between the priest's house and the church.

The association's general secretary, M.J. O'Lehane, who was due in Limerick later that week as a member of the congress executive, said they had sent £200 to their Limerick branch secretary. He anticipated that they would send a very substantial sum to the strike committee itself.

Impressive though some of these amounts may sound, they came nowhere near the £7,000-£8,000 a week it was calculated would be needed to keep the strike going. At the end of ten days, it was estimated £1,000 had been received in Limerick, and some days later that figure had increased to only £1,500.

Throughout nationalist Ireland there was strong support among political bodies. The second biggest financial donation, £500, came from the Mansion House conference. At a large demonstration in Cavan, to welcome home a Sinn Féin TD, released from internment, a resolution was passed unanimously congratulating the Limerick citizens on their magnificent fight against English militarism and pledging them moral and material support. The TD, Peadar Galligan, said no attempt to create a breach between Labour and Sinn Féin would succeed.

In Co. Westmeath, Mullingar Rural District Council adopted a resolution congratulating the workers of Limerick on their fight against oppression. North Tipperary Sinn Féin Executive appealed to all clubs in the constituency for potatoes, oatmeal, eggs and other foodstuffs for the relief of Limerick. The chairman of Limerick County Council wrote to the authorities protesting at the restrictions, and two members said they could not attend a council meeting because they refused to ask for permission from anyone to discharge their duties as elected public representatives. Cork Guardians also passed a resolution of condemnation and pledged support for Limerick. At this meeting, controversy broke out over the role of the National Union of Railwaymen. The motion had been moved by John Good, the local secretary of the NUR. He was criticised by D. Williams for pretending it was a labour matter, and trying to get Sinn Féin involved, while at the same time "he took care to carry out the orders of his master in England, Mr Thomas". [4]

Traditionally, the annual congress of the Gaelic Athletic Association is held at Easter. As at the trade union conferences held around that time, a Limerick delegate moved to get support for the strike. Newspaper reports differ as to whether, in this case, the speaker was an ordinary delegate or someone sent to represent the strike committee. Again, however, he gave an insight into how well the soviet was coping. The workers were as well fed as at any time in their lives; they were getting milk at the right price and potatoes for nearly nothing. No distress had occurred so far, but the strike committee wanted to have funds in hand for any unforeseen eventualities. Two prominent Republicans, Harry Boland and J.J. Walsh, proposed and seconded a resolution to grant £100 to the strike funds from the Association. A delegate from the Munster council of the GAA pledged ten pounds, and after other delegates had pledged money, a collection on the spot realised over thirty pounds.

As a sports organisation, the GAA offered help in the most practical way it could. Four matches were arranged to raise money for the strike fund. At the association's headquarters in Croke Park, Louth would play Dublin in Gaelic football, and in another football game at Roscommon, Galway were matched against Roscommon. Two hurling matches were arranged. At Cork, the home county would play Tipperary, and Cork would travel to Tralee to play Kerry.

The delegates baulked at the suggestion of playing the games on May Day. Whatever about protesting at the situation in Limerick, they clearly drew the line at anything that smacked of "Socialism" or "Politics". The Gaelic football game at Croke Park drew between 3,000 and 4,000 spectators. It is difficult to judge whether this was evidence of widespread support for the strike or merely a reflection of the popularity of the fixture. Dublin, in any event, defeated Louth comprehensively, by a goal and seven points to a single point.

Further afield, in Britain, the advanced left were in support. At the Independent Labour Party conference, in Huddersfield, councillor Cradford, of Edinburgh, said they ought to do something to encourage "The Limerick Soviet". He would like to see the working classes of Great Britain following the soviet's example in offering a paper currency of their own. [5] Cradford said they were with their Irish friends in spirit against the military regime. The future prime minister of Britain, Ramsay MacDonald, opposed the strike, declaring that the nearest thing to a "Soviet" in Britain was the House of Lords! Cradford retorted that the Limerick soviet was the first working-class soviet on practical lines established in the British isles. But the conference was so divided on the issue that no vote was taken.

The *Irish Times* noted what it called the "injurious praise" of the Independent Labour Party and the British Socialist Party. The Socialist Party's annual conference, in Sheffield, passed a resolution wishing success to their fellow-workers of Limerick in their struggle for civil liberty. Cathal O'Shannon, a prominent official of the ITGWU and a leading light in the Socialist Party of Ireland, made a fiery speech. To laughter, O'Shannon said it was bad enough having to work without having to get a permit to do so. If a general strike was called, he said, it would not end with a Limerick soviet. To cheers, he predicted it might end with something more than the British occupation of Ireland would want to stomach.

O'Shannon said, if necessary, arrangements could be made for a general strike, including James Thomas's railway men. He said he looked to a combination of the elements of the left in Scotland and south Wales, Ireland and England, which would bring about an alliance of revolutionary socialists and end what he termed "the white terror" now prevailing.

The Workers' Socialist Federation dispatched a correspondent to Limerick to report at first hand for its newspaper, *The Workers' Dreadnought*, edited by the noted women's rights activist Sylvia Pankhurst. The *Dreadnought* later carried a series of articles entitled "The Truth about the Limerick Soviet" and their reporter filed graphic, harrowing accounts of the conditions under which women workers, in particular, were employed in the city. [6]

One of the first acts of the joint meeting of the strike committee and congress executive in Limerick was to send a telegram to the Scottish Trade Union Congress, then meeting in Perth. This rather combative telegram read: "Limerick workers for nine days have been on strike against the veto placed upon their movement by your military authorities. Your servants, the army of occupation here, refuse to allow the citizens to proceed to and from their daily work, except under military permit. Limerick workers refuse to submit to this indignity and sign of subjugation. You, Scottish workers, cannot absolve yourselves from responsibility unless you take action immediately." [7]

The following day, the Scottish TUC responded with a unanimous resolution demanding the withdrawal of the embargo on the workers of Limerick. [8] W.B. MacMahon of the Railway Clerks' Association was the Irish fraternal delegate to the TUC and he reported the decision to the Irish newspapers. But Mr Allan, secretary of the TUC, also forwarded a telegram of protest to the chief secretary for Ireland in Dublin Castle. [9] This was not the only telegram or letter of protest from Britain to land on MacPherson's desk. The executive council of the United Operative Plumbers and Domestic Engineers Association had discussed the strike at their general office in Newcastle-on-Tyne. [10] In an emphatic letter of protest from their assistant general secretary, Lachlan MacDonald, they said they were of the opinion that the circumstances in Limerick did not warrant such drastic curtailment of the citizens' rights and that there must be other means that could be adopted.

The secretary of the Dennistoun branch of the Independent Labour Party – a person with the Irish-sounding name of P. Lavin – forwarded a resolution passed at a "largely-attended" meeting of the branch.[11] They protested "in the strongest possible way against the barbarous methods of repression resorted to by the British Government in Co. Limerick and other parts of Ireland" and they called for the immediate withdrawal from Ireland of all British troops.

Another unmistakably Irish name was on the letter of protest from the Merthyr and Dowlais Sinn Féin Club, in south Wales. [12] Signed by J. Crowley, and sent to the home secretary in Whitehall, this again called for the withdrawal of troops from Ireland, and condemned "the treatment meted out to the people of Limerick by the military authorities". Ealing Labour Party and Trades Council unanimously adopted a resolution protesting strongly against "the isolation and military coercion of the inhabitants of the City of Limerick" and demanding the withdrawal of troops from the city and the ending of the proclaimed area. [13]

But if nationalist Ireland stood firmly with Limerick, the Unionist workers of north-east Ulster remained aloof and suspicious. Ninety percent of the skilled trades unionists in Ireland were employed in Belfast's factories and shipyards. The Belfast correspondent of the *Daily Telegraph* reported: "A strong line against the proposed national strike of Irish unions has been taken by organised labour in Belfast ... The Limerick dispute being Sinn Féin in origin, the workers in Belfast have intimated they will be no party to the strike, and if the Irish Trade Union Congress or any other body calls for a cessation of work the order will be ignored. Local district committees of British trade unions have been warned they must not use funds for the proposed Irish strike" [14] The correspondent noted that this would be similar to what had happened early in 1918 during the anti-conscription strike, when Belfast had continued working though Dublin and the South was at a standstill.

The Protestant workers of north-east Ulster remained implacably opposed to Irish independence. They had long feared what they foresaw as their submersion in a society dominated by priests and peasants. They regarded the Irish Labour Party and Trade Union Congress as little more than the industrial wing of Sinn Féin, dedicated to the establishment of Bolshevism throughout Ireland. A Unionist MP, Thomas Donald, told a meeting of electors in Belfast's Victoria division that he could not see any difference between the people they knew as Bolshevists in Russia and those who were creating the present situation in the south of Ireland. This stance faced the trade union leadership with the impossible dilemma of trying to maintain organisational unity across the island of Ireland in the face of a diversity of economic and political interests between North and South.

Sharing a common religious outlook with their employers, in a society where many Catholics did not recognise the legitimacy or authority of the government, Protestant workers monopolised the skilled and best-paid jobs and acquiesced in sectarian discrimination against Catholics. The North's major industries depended heavily on the imperial link for their continued prosperity, and Protestant workers feared for their jobs, prosperity and privileges in an independent Ireland pursuing protectionist trade policies. Thus, a combination of economic interest and sectarian differences kept the Protestant workers hostile to the independence movement.

The period from the end of the 1880s to 1914 failed to produce a trade union movement throughout Ireland that was united in its political as well as its industrial aims. That was so, despite the development during that time, in Britain and Ireland, of the more militant "new unionism" and events like Jim Larkin's union of Protestant and Catholic workers during the great Belfast Docks Strike of 1907.

Three factors combined to identify Catholic workers with Fenian nationalism. The mass mobilisation of nationalists under Parnell, and Orange resistance to Home Rule had equated Irishness with Catholicism. The tension between the two sections of the working-class was intensified by the systematic exclusion of Catholics from skilled Ulster trades, and the political radicalism of the leaders of "new unionism" was regarded with suspicion by the Ulster's Protestant craftsmen.

The trade union organisation of previously unorganised, unskilled workers – largely Catholic – at a time of increasing political tension over the link with Britain served to divide, rather than to unite, the working-class. It became impossible to construct a labour movement that was both political and industrial and that united Protestant and Catholic, Orange and Green. It might have been possible if the existing division between craft and non-craft, skilled and unskilled did not also follow the sectarian divide between Protestant and Catholic.

A united trade union movement was possible only insofar as it did not involve itself in the question of the link with Britain, in other words, by ignoring the dominant issue in Irish politics. With the exception of James Connolly, this is what the Labour leadership did in practice. Connolly, in effect, played the Green card. He opted for a labour movement that appealed essentially to southerners and Catholics. This might be justified on the basis that the majority of Irish people were Catholics and the Catholic working class may have appeared to be more promising material for social revolution than their Protestant counterparts. But Connolly's decision finally excluded the possibility of a united, political movement of all Irish workers. It meant the equation, and ultimate subordination, of southern Irish labour to Irish nationalism.

In practice, after Connolly's death, trade union leaders like William O'Brien and Thomas Johnson accepted this position and they did not allow events like the Limerick soviet to threaten trade union organisational unity throughout the island of Ireland. The syndicalist orientation of Irish Labour, with its emphasis on industrial aims and means – as opposed to politics – made it all the easier for the leadership to adopt this stance.

An extensive special debate on Limerick at the annual congress of the Irish National Teachers' Organisation, held in University Buildings, Dublin, is worth looking at in some detail for what it reveals of Northern attitudes. The national teachers had a wide membership in all parts of the country. Their debate was spread over two days, starting on Thursday, 24 April, the day the partial resumption of work was decided on in Limerick.

George O'Callaghan, a delegate from Newcastle West, in Co. Limerick, moved the suspension of standing orders to "draw attention to the fact that several of our colleagues are unable to pursue their work at the present time". [15] Standing orders were raised to allow discussion of a motion pledging support to the workers of Limerick but when it became clear that discussion on this would be heated, the matter was left over until the following day. O'Callaghan said there was no question of politics involved, people of all shades of politics were united in Limerick. He appealed to the delegates to make some return for their alliance with Labour. A Co. Clare delegate warned that if the national teachers were capable of turning their backs on Labour he would leave the organisation the next day.

A succession of Northern delegates opposed O'Callaghan. McNallis from Dungannon, Co. Tyrone, said they, in the North, could always work on organisation matters without causing a word of friction. Why was it, he asked, that it was only when they met in congress from different parts of Ireland that a jarring note was sounded. Was it not evident that matters were introduced that should be left alone? McNallis continued: "No one who had read that day's papers could have any difficulty in deciding whether this was a political matter or not. This did not begin as a Labour question. If it were purely a Labour question, there would be no difficulty about the delegates throwing in their lot with Labour, but I submit it was not purely a Labour question." [16]

McNallis's next comments exposed how susceptible to rupture was the fragile unity of the Northern and southern members once a "political" issue was raised. According to the *Irish Independent* report, "When it was said that this would lead to secession of branches in the North, someone said 'Small Loss!', but he would remind them there was a time when they were glad to have the men from the North to plead their cause." [17]

Another Co. Tyrone delegate, Ramsay, of Cookstown, said he could not yet see that the matter was dissociated from politics. The proclamation issued in Limerick stated that they were on strike as a protest against the ban on the city – not on the ban against going to work. He placed the organisation above everything, and knowing that this matter interfered with the organisation, he would oppose it. Ramsay said he did not think the time had arrived when the teachers of Ireland would be convinced that this was not a political problem.

The spectre of the partition of Ireland was raised in the speech of another Northern delegate, Stanage, from Banbridge in Co. Down. He appealed to the teachers' congress to think very seriously before pushing the resolution. They wanted a united Ireland, but were they going to have the first partition an educational one, and were they going to give a handle to others to put them in a peculiar position? A delegate called Judge made a similar plea not to drive a wedge between the North and the South. Had the delegates received instructions from their associations on how to vote on a question that might split the congress and lead to the setting up of breakaway unions? he asked.

Speakers from Republican heartlands like Counties Kilkenny and Tipperary were dismissive of these arguments in their contributions. The Kilkenny delegate, Frisby, appealed to the teachers to "stick to Labour and to stick to Limerick". [18] If the Scottish Trade Union Congress were not afraid to call for the withdrawal of the military embargo, why should the teachers be afraid to, he asked. They had heard of partition on the subject of education in the North of Ireland, and that policy had found its most influential supporters in the ranks of their members in Belfast. Cries of "Wrong!" greeted this remark.

Mansfield, from Tipperary, was even more dismissive of Northern anxieties and appeals for unity. "They were all anxious for unity," Mansfield said, "and no threat of cleavage had been made if the motion which had been brought forward by the Limerick delegates failed. Unity was very good, but if it came to a question of principle, then let them scrap unity." He protested against the bogey of unity being brought forward to cow the majority, who were entitled on democratic grounds to rule any organised body. "Let them have unity, but let principle, right and justice prevail, he declared, even if the organisation went bang." [19]

In the end, a compromise resolution was carried. [20] This referred the question of support for Limerick to the union's central executive council, to await the outcome of the expected special Trade Union Congress. Thus the Northern delegates had their sensibilities respected on the day, but for the Southern delegates the resolution also committed the central executive council to "act in harmony" with the decision of any trade union congress.

INTO sensitivity on an issue like Limerick was understandable. As far back as 1916, in the wake of the Easter rising, Unionist teachers had set up the Irish

Protestant National Teachers' Union (IPNTU), a body that remained closely aligned to the INTO. In June 1916, the IPNTU had set up a sub-committee to "watch Protestant teachers' interests in the so-called Irish question". The decision was followed by a loyal toast and the singing of "God Save the King". Resolutions of sympathy passed by INTO branches and by the union's central committee in the aftermath of the rising and the internment of its participants, led to further friction with the IPNTU. The tensions increased following the national teachers' decision, in 1917, to affiliate to what the president of the IPNTU called the "frankly Bolshevist and Sinn Féin" Irish Labour Party and Trade Union Congress. The ILPTUC's opposition to conscription, and the decision to withdraw in favour of Sinn Féin in the 1918 general election, led to Northern Protestant resignations from the INTO. By the time of the INTO congress of 1919, branches in Coleraine, Lisburn, Derry and Newtownards had left the union. Later that year, on 19 July, the final breach was made when the Ulster National Teachers' Union was formed.

The sensitivity of Northern Loyalists in the trade unions on any question that smacked of nationalism or separatism was further underlined during the period of the Limerick strike by a controversy over a call from the Irish Trade Union Congress to suspend work on Labour Day, 1 May 1919, and to celebrate it as an unpaid holiday.

The call was made in a poster, signed by the Irish TUC general secretary, William O'Brien, and displayed in Dublin, declaring that the workers of Ireland had decided to celebrate 1 May, Labour Day, as a general holiday, and that all work would be suspended that day "to demonstrate that the Irish working class joins with the international Labour movement in demanding a democratic League of Free Nations as the necessary condition of a permanent peace based upon the self-determination of all peoples, including the people of Ireland". [21] For Ulster Unionists, the sting was in the tail of that resolution. Once again, as in the case of Limerick, the attitude of the National Union of Railwaymen and their general secretary James Thomas was crucial. Irish railwaymen seemed willing to join in the stoppage. The call to stop work was supported by the Irish Railway Workers' Emergency Committee, representing the NUR, the Railway Clerks' Association, the Amalgamated Society of Engineers, the ITGWU and the railway craft unions. But, on instructions from London, the Irish secretary of the NUR, Rimmer, issued a directive to all his branches that they were not to absent themselves from work on 1 May without the sanction of their executive committee.

For the Irish TUC, William O'Brien made a typically scathing reply. He pointed out that it was Rimmer himself, on behalf of the NUR, who had proposed a resolution at the 1917 congress calling on them to seek to establish an international Labour Day. The resolution had been seconded by two NUR members and adopted by congress. Now, according to O'Brien, the TUC was merely acting on that resolution and therefore the attitude of Thomas, as general secretary of the NUR, was hard to understand. He pointed out that Thomas himself had been at the International Trade Union Conference in Berne that nominated 1 May as Labour Day.

A writer to the *Irish Independent*, signing himself "Trade Unionist", was less impressed by the deliberations of the Berne conference. [22] He preferred the idea of celebrating Labour Day on a Sunday, when no loss of pay would be involved, and in something of a non-sequitur he asked – in the name of democracy: "What is the Berne Conference doing for the Limerick workers?"

Three branches of the NUR in Cork, representing over a thousand workers, rejected Rimmer's instructions and decided to stick by their decision to stop work on May Day. The Bray no. 2 branch of the union made a similar decision, making it clear they were following the wishes of the Irish TUC in doing so. But in Derry, Loyalist workers refused to take part in a planned demonstration, believing Sinn Féin to be behind the proposed cessation of work. The "No Surrender" band turned down an invitation from the Derry Trades and Labour Council to celebrate Labour Day. The band's reply pointed out that practically all of its members had joined the colours, while those running the Labour Day demonstration were associated in the protest against conscription. Consequently, as loyal subjects, the band declined to have anything to do with the turnout.

The executive committee of the Londonderry branch of the Ulster Unionist Labour Association decided to request all their members, and all Protestant workers, male and female, not to take part in the May Day demonstration. They warned it was "of a revolutionary and Bolshevik nature and supported by Sinn Féin propagandists, as already stated at the opening of Dail Eireann and that honest labour should repudiate such actions". [23]

Derry Loyalists, believing there was a strong Sinn Féin influence at work, were particularly aggrieved that it was proposed to assemble at the Mall Wall, close to the Derry Apprentice Boys' Memorial Hall. A similar proposal, in the past, had led to rioting.

May Day 1919 repeated the pattern of the 1918 national strike against conscription and was a harbinger of the coming split between North and South. In nationalist Ireland, there were demonstrations of record sizes and the red flag was carried even in small towns. The resolutions adopted emphasised world peace, the self-determination of nations and the call for May Day to be a public holiday. The call for a stoppage of work was responded to almost everywhere. The exceptions were Belfast and North East Ulster and the city of Limerick.

After the rigours of the fortnight-long general strike, Limerick was an understandable exception. The trades council decided against a May Day stoppage because, they said, it would "not be fair to stop work". As work resumed in all Limerick factories on Monday, 28 April, the trades council met to decide its attitude to the proposed May Day stoppage. Some representatives of the ITGWU urged that May Day be observed, but the majority view was against another work stoppage so soon after the sacrifices made during the soviet. [24]

Four days after May Day, the newspapers carried reports that the proclamation of a portion of the city of Limerick as a special military area, from April 9, was withdrawn. [25] Permits were no longer necessary and there was free access to the city.

Epilogue

"Unless they were prepared to use the guns and hoist the Red Flag from one end of the country to the other there was no use in condemning the National Executive because they did not call a General Strike."
Walter Carpenter, delegate of the International Tailors' Union, at the Irish Labour Party and Trade Union Congress, 1919.

"It is entirely a Labour question. The right to come and go without having to get military permits is involved. The attitude of the workers is completely misrepresented and misunderstood by endeavouring to show that the situation is in any way connected with politics".
John Cronin, Chairman, Limerick Strike Committee, Irish Independent, 23 April 1919.

" ... a general strike is an effective weapon of defence, no doubt, but we have an even more effective weapon in our hands and we should not hesitate to use it for the sake of justice."
Patrick O'Connor, in the newspaper "An tEireannach", 3 May, 1919.

The Irish Labour Party and Trade Union Congress held a major debate on Limerick at its annual congress in Drogheda, in August 1919. [1] It is a good starting point for any analysis and evaluation of the strike.

The first criticism of the congress's handling of the strike came from Michael O'Donnell, a delegate of the Irish Clerical Workers' Union, who was a member of the Limerick strike committee. He felt that the national executive had not done everything that should have been done: "The Limerick strikers were let down by someone." [2] O'Donnell criticised the executive's delay in travelling to Limerick. He said that a special congress should have been held *before* they travelled to the city and that the delay had "allowed certain undercurrents to get to work to sap and undermine the movement in Limerick."

This point was echoed by a Cork delegate, named O'Duffy, who claimed the strike had ended as a result of "subterranean influences". [3] A Typographical Society delegate from Dublin, O'Flanagan, tried to deflect criticism of the national executive on to the headquarters of the British trade unions. According to O'Flanagan, the strike was a direct challenge by the workers to the military tyranny that existed in Ireland. British Labour did not support them because it had been reported in the press there that the strike was a Sinn Féin movement.

It was in the interests of Labour generally for British trade unionists to come to the rescue of Irish Labour. But if it came to a question of "direct action" and they expected support from the other side, British trade unionists would let them down. William O'Brien, the congress general secretary, made a typically acerbic, but masterly, intervention in the debate. O'Brien had a long and multi-facetted career in the Labour movement; he held most of the major positions in the congress and the ITGWU; he was a close friend and confidant of James Connolly; his great achievements were mainly organisational but were often marked by bitter clashes with former colleagues like Big Jim Larkin and P.T. Daly.

O'Brien set out in detail the telegrams, consultations and meetings that had been the congress's early response to the events in Limerick. He explained the difficulties in getting the entire executive to Limerick at the earliest possible date, because of the pressure of other work on some key members. O'Brien was immediately followed by speakers from Cork and King's County (now Offaly) who accepted his explanation.

Then came another Limerick delegate, James O'Connor, secretary of Limerick trades council. The official conference report continues: "Coming from Limerick and speaking for the workers there, he declared that Limerick was not let down. [Applause.] They held they made the greatest fight ever made by any united body of workers in a big city. They showed the world that the workers were able to run the city in spite of the presence of any foreign Government. They held they won in Limerick [applause] and they blamed nobody for letting them down. They fought their own fight with the help of the Executive and fought well." O'Connor then handed in a copy of the last proclamation issued by the strike committee.[4]

Another effective defence of the executive came from Thomas Farren, the congress vice-president. While he agreed that the strike was a "glorious triumph" for the organised workers of Limerick, Farren said that they had made one mistake. They should not have declared a strike for an indefinite period.[5] If they had declared a strike for a week, they would have accomplished as much.

On the question of declaring a national stoppage, Farren said that while the national leadership had agreed that a national conference might be called, they made it clear that if they did call a national stoppage it would be only a demonstration for a few days as "they realised that under the present state of affairs they were not prepared for the Revolution."

This lack of preparation for a revolutionary challenge was the nub of the congress dilemma. It was a theme taken up in a persuasive way in a contribution from Walter Carpenter, a delegate from the International Tailors, Dublin. Carpenter said he spoke as someone who was an advocate of the general strike, but the national executive could not have taken any action other than what they did.

Carpenter continued: "He knew what the General Strike meant – that it has got to be backed up by guns, that it meant a Revolution; and until they were prepared for Revolution there was no use calling a General Strike. Unless they were prepared to use the guns and hoist the Red Flag from one end of the country to the other there was no use in condemning the National Executive because they did not call a General Strike." [6]

According to the Tailors' delegate, the workers were not class conscious enough, not educated enough and not ready for a general strike. But when the day came that they were class conscious and educated, the workers would not want leaders – they would go out themselves. Carpenter hoped the day would soon come when they would be ready for the general strike, "when they would be able to put in practice in Ireland what they had done in Russia and establish a Soviet Republic [applause]." [7]

It was now time for Johnson himself to give an account of the executive's stewardship. He believed the Limerick committee were right to act quickly – without consulting the executive – if their action was to be of any effect. There were times when local people must take on themselves the responsibility for doing things and taking the consequences, and this, he asserted, was one of them. But due consideration must be given to any suggestion of an enormous extension of the local action.

They could never win a strike by downing tools against the British Army, Johnson declared. [8] It was for them as an executive to decide whether this was the moment to act in Ireland, whether there was a probability of a response in England and Scotland. Their knowledge of those countries did not lead them to think that any big action in Ireland would have brought a responsive movement there.

"A general strike could have been legitimately called in Ireland on twelve occasions during the past two years", Johnson continued, "but it was not a question of justification. It was a question of strategy. Were they to take the enemy's time or were they to take their own?" They knew that if the railwaymen came out the soldiers would have taken on the railways the next day. They knew that if the soldiers were put on the railways, the railways would have been blown up. They knew that would have meant armed revolt.

"Did they as Trade Unionists suggest that it was for their Executive to say such action should be taken at a particular time, knowing, assured as they were, that it would have resulted in armed revolt in Ireland?" he asked. There might be an occasion to decide on a down tools policy which would have the effect of calling out the armed forces of the crown, but "Limerick was not the occasion … Let them remember what the strike was. It was a protest and the Limerick Committee emphasised the fact, against a military tyranny."

By implication, Johnson's speech makes it clear that the proposal of a national congress, put to the Limerick strike committee, was never really taken seriously by the congress executive, unless the outcome was to be a token, national stoppage as mentioned by Farren. Johnson's speech illustrates that for all the "syndicalist" rhetoric of the Irish trade union movement they had neither the politics nor the organisation needed to challenge British state power in Ireland.

The pivotal role of the railwaymen, outlined by Johnson, was gone into in some detail in the Drogheda debate. Six different delegates, including Michael Keyes from the Limerick Branch of the NUR, defended their position. Davin, from Dublin, said the railway workers were right to get the views of their national executive and consider their position before rushing into action.

Larkin, of Waterford, and an NUR delegate from Cork, John Good, said they were ready to take action when called on. Good said that they could not get in touch with Limerick for two days, to see what was going on. He believed the military authorities had tampered with their correspondence and they were therefore anxious not to give away information to the enemy. Good had been in a position to call out his members in Cork, but he felt it was unwise to take such action until they knew definitely what was going on in Limerick, including the origin and cause of the dispute.

Once the Cork railwaymen knew the facts of the situation, they instructed Good that they would down tools in support of Limerick whether the London executive of the NUR liked it or not. Normally, they would follow their executive, but they felt they understood conditions in Ireland better, Good said. Another NUR delegate, and a member of the congress executive, T.C.Daly, rose to defend the rail workers' position. It was the first time in his memory, he said, that a charge had been made against the railwaymen of failing to respond to the call of Labour. Was it not the railwaymen who had originated the movement that defeated conscription? And now they were told by cowardly innuendo that the railwaymen had let down the workers of Limerick! He said, standing there representing the railwaymen, that he had only to get the word from the national executive to press the button and the railwaymen would have answered the call [applause].

Daly's speech goes to the heart of why the might of the National Union of Railwaymen – the power to paralyse communications – had not come into play on the side of Limerick. It was not any lack of willingness on the part of their rank-and-file, but rather the caution of the national trade union leadership in the face of what they foresaw as the inevitable consequences of such action.

When the section of the annual report dealing with Limerick was put to the congress it was adopted with only one vote against. That came from the delegate of King's County (Offaly) trades council, Smyth.[9] But he never spoke on this issue, so we can only speculate on his reasons for opposing the section. For British trade union leaders, such as the National Union of Railwaymen, one of

The Great Southern and Western railway's engineering shop at Limerick. Members of the Amalgamated Society of Engineers employed here supported the soviet, but the caution and lack of commitment of their National Union of Railwaymen colleagues ensured its defeat.

the difficulties – or excuses – in dealing with Limerick was in deciding whether it was a type of industrial stoppage or some kind of "political" action. In the conventional wisdom of the British unions, political power was pursued through political parties and, therefore, trade unions did not involve themselves in "political" actions. It was the "political" nature of the Limerick strike that was seized upon by J.H.Thomas and the NUR as their reason for withholding official sanction.

The syndicalist legacy of Connolly in the Irish trade union movement meant that they were probably less rigorous in maintaining that distinction. The widespread overlapping of membership between the trade unions and advanced nationalist organisations also helped to blur the distinction between industrial and political, at least on this side of the Irish Sea.

The gulf between Irish and British trade unionism was a wide one. An Irish nationalist's "industrial" strike might be an Englishman's "political" action, yet both were simply looking at the same events from a different perspective. From the Limerick strike onwards, the British trade unions – especially the National Union of Railwaymen – were consistently cool in their attitude towards "political" strikes in Ireland. The requests and actions of the Irish members were drowned in a welter of rule-books, bureaucracy and procrastinating executive council decisions. As the *New Statesman* put it, "a certain measure of academic approval was forthcoming, but active support was lacking from the first".[10]

It was the British intelligentsia, rather than its workers or trade union leaders, who were most deeply opposed to the government's repressive policies and who felt they were contrary to British traditions of public and political life. Perhaps if the trade unions had taken direct action it would have given substance to the accusation that extremists in the British Labour movement were in alliance with the "Sinn Féin Bolsheviks" in Ireland. That, in turn, might have alienated the kind of respectable people who were active in bodies like the Peace with Ireland Council. They sympathised with Ireland's plight but did not wish to be party to a revolutionary upsurge aimed at overturning society in the British Isles.

The difference between British and Irish trade union attitudes may also be explained by the differing roles of trade union centres in colonial or quasi-colonial countries compared with centres in metropolitan or imperialist countries. In an imperialist country, like Britain, part of the standard of living of trade unionists depended on the availability of cheap raw materials from the colonies, the restriction of colonial competition and the enforced freedom of trade for finished goods in the colonies. To that extent, there was common economic cause between the trade unions and the empire's business people. For many trade unionists in the old imperial states of Europe, making common cause with oppressed workers in the colonies meant, to an extent, jeopardising their own standard of living because it put their employers' profits at risk. And the Labour movements of Europe – including Britain – were far from immune to sentiments of jingoism and chauvinism where "national" interests were concerned, as the events after the outbreak of World War I illustrated.

This partly explains the reluctance of the powerful British trade unions to weigh in on the side of the Limerick strikers. But there was a further compelling reason. At this time, probably over seventy percent of Irish trade unionists were members of British trade unions, but most of that membership was concentrated in the Loyalist section of north east Ulster. Inevitably, any words or actions that smacked of support for Irish separatism would fall foul of those members. In their desire to retain their Ulster membership, the British unions were severely constrained in how far they could go in support of actions taken by their members in the rest of Ireland.

A great deal of the propaganda, for and against the Limerick strike, therefore, was centred on this issue of whether it was a "Labour" or a "political" phenomenon. "Political" in this sense meant not so much to do with politics in a party sense, but with the political questions of Irish nationalism, Irish self-determination and Irish separatism. Often, for tactical reasons, in order to secure or maintain British Labour support, the strike's supporters stressed that it was a "labour" question. In trying to grapple with this dilemma, Tom Johnson said it was political, "but only in the sense that the fight against conscription was political".[11]

Unwittingly, Johnson had put his finger on the nub of the problem for the British unions. Ulster Loyalist trade unionists had refused to support the anti-conscription campaign for the precise reason that they viewed it as damaging to their political interest in retaining a constitutional link with Britain. If Limerick was "political" in the same sense, there was no question of support for the strike in Loyalist Ulster. On the other hand, people like Johnson could not pursue the "non-political" line so far that they alienated possible support from middle-class and farming supporters of Irish nationalism in the rest of Ireland.

Opponents, like the *Irish Times* and unionist politicians in Ulster, portrayed Limerick as a Sinn Féin strike and emphasised what they saw as a Republican role in organising and maintaining it. A week into the strike, the *Irish Times* claimed shrewd judges detected the guiding hand of Sinn Féin in ensuring that the strike committee's functions were carried out with a thoroughness that was uncharacteristic of provincial strikes up to then. [12] Though there was no open alliance, the newspaper conceded, there was a complete accord between the political and industrial parties. "Defiance of British law affords them a common platform", the *Irish Times* claimed. But, the same report said, Labour took care ostensibly to keep itself aloof from politics lest it should offend its friends in Great Britain. The paper reported seeing very few emblems of Sinn Féin, and except for the daubing of the Treaty Stone in Republican colours there was "no glaring display" of the tricolour. Many Sinn Féiners, apparently, had decided to remain within the proscribed area rather than apply for military permits and had even resisted the temptation to spend Easter by the seaside rather than submit to the indignity of applying.

When John Cronin was asked for his reaction to the refusals of the NUR and the British TUC to lend official support, he claimed there was "nothing whatever political" – that is, nothing to do with nationalism – in the protest on behalf of the workers of Limerick. "It is entirely a Labour question," he said. "The right to come and go without having to get military permits is involved. The attitude of the workers is completely misrepresented and misunderstood by endeavouring to show that the situation is in any way connected with politics."

In his memoir of the strike, the trades council treasurer, James Casey, indicates that much of the supply of food for Limerick, from outside, was organised by the IRA and smuggled past the military cordon. The *Observer*'s correspondent in Ireland, the writer Captain Stephen Gwynn, saw Limerick as having been started by the "Labour wing" of Sinn Féin, but saw the ending of the strike as a defeat for the whole of Sinn Féin and a triumph for the military.[13] Gwynn praised both the military and the soviet for their wise and capable handling of events. The nationalist newspaper *New Ireland*, writing some days after the strike ended seemed dismissive of any trade union lessons that might have been learned, but saw the chief value of the strike in "the effect it will have in putting the energetic nationalists on their mettle."[14] The *Irish Times* noted the refusal of the British trade unions to accept that the strike had no connection with "politics", but was merely Irish Labour's challenge to assaults on its dignity and convenience.[15] The newspaper believed that the strike had escalated from being a purely local affair to being used as a deliberate and very ambitious attack on the whole system of Irish government. It could no longer be dissociated from the propaganda of the Irish Republicans, and the involvement of the Trade Union Congress, promising to extend the strike nationally, was an attempt to bring the whole nation to a social and economic standstill.

So far as the strikers saw matters, Limerick was more concerned with making a sustained protest against intolerable conditions locally, than with being the precursor of a national challenge to the British government. From early on, the national trade union leadership made it clear they were not prepared to offer such a challenge, at least not without the support or the blessing of Sinn Féin, the Volunteers and the Dáil. The Limerick strike was the first open challenge to British rule since the separatist Dáil was established but, in the end, it proved no match for the government.

After the strike ended, there were bitter recriminations and criticism of the strike leaders in Limerick from Republican newspapers, proving how brittle had been their alliance with organised Labour. The comments showed little appreciation of the difficult organisational, let alone political, issues that would have faced the unions if they had decided to continue the strike. A Republican broadsheet poured scorn on leaders who had "bowed the knee in shameful submission to the army of occupation". The paper claimed the people had been let down by "the nincompoops who call themselves the 'Leaders of Labour' in Limerick", and the end of the strike had come as a "death blow" to the hopes of the people.[16]

The real attitude of militant Republicans to trade union action may have been betrayed in these scornful comments of Patrick O'Connor, writing in the newspaper *An tEireannach* (The Irishman): " ... a general strike is an effective weapon of defence, no doubt, but we have an even more effective weapon in our hands and we should not hesitate to use it for the sake of justice." [17] The workers of Limerick were so exhausted, especially financially, after the strike ended that the trades council voted not to observe Labour Day on 1 May. Some workers had received strike pay from their unions, or had even been paid by employers who had Republican sympathies. But many others had received nothing, and some had not been reinstated after the strike ended. It was estimated that £25,000 was needed to alleviate distress, but the strike fund closed after two weeks, holding just over £17,000. At the annual conference of the ILPTUC, some unions complained that their donations had not been registered in the fund. Many other donations reported in the newspapers do not appear to have been recorded, more likely because of organisational pressures than because of any dishonesty. Nevertheless, the total amount subscribed to help Limerick, while larger than the amount recorded, still fell far short of what was needed.

In early May, the ILPTUC national executive issued a rather perfunctory appeal for help for Limerick, in a circular asking for "some financial assistance to be rendered to them". At a meeting of Dublin trades council on 5 May, when the circular was discussed, some members of the national executive were less than enthusiastic. Thomas Farren enquired how much the executive itself had given, and was told, amid laughter, by another executive member that they had "given their moral support".[18] William O'Brien himself was against a council subscription, saying it should be left up to individual unions. His remarks made him extremely unpopular in Limerick. A Limerick worker wrote to the Dublin *Saturday Post* describing the executive's evacuation plan as the most ridiculous suggestion since "Moses struck the rock".[19] He was particularly critical of the executive's failure to go to Limerick immediately and demanded to know why the general secretary had not gone there.

The aftermath of the strike brought bitterness and division to Limerick trades council itself. At the best of times, there had been an uneasy relationship between the old-style craft unions and the new industrial unionism of the ITGWU. The post-strike debates allowed full scope for that latent antagonism to flourish. At national level, both the ITGWU itself and the Irish TUC were wracked by a bitter rivalry between William O'Brien – representing safe, rule-book trade unionism – and P.T. Daly, who seemed to represent militancy and greater rank-and-file power.

These national factions had their local Limerick followers. The stance taken for or against the national executive's actions during the strike became a litmus test of where loyalties lay on the national rivalry of O'Brien and Daly. What were ostensibly procedural, or constitutional questions, such as the number of delegates to be sent to the Drogheda conference, became the focus of conflict between skilled and unskilled, between the ITGWU favouring a strong, centralised union movement and the craft unions which preferred a more local, less rigid organisational structure.

As a carpenter himself, the council chairman, John Cronin, was firmly opposed to the ITGWU line and did not want to oppose or embarrass the national executive. He said: "everyone knows the facts of Limerick, and the Council wants no capital made out of it."[20] He announced that the trades council's report on the strike would not be ready before the Drogheda conference, thus avoiding the possibility that any negative comments would be seized on by delegates opposed to the leadership.

A wrangle over the delegates for Drogheda left Limerick represented by two Transport Union members, with Cronin refusing to attend and failing to take up a nomination for the vice presidency of the Trade Union Congress. The nomination for the vice presidency was probably intended to honour Cronin for his leadership of the Limerick strike but it would also disarm him as a potential critic of the national leadership. The Drogheda conference faced him with a dilemma. As leader of the strike he would have wanted to criticise the national executive, but as a craftsman he knew this would play into the hands of the Left faction, whom he opposed.

Daly's followers held public meetings and declared they would crush O'Brien and Johnson at the congress. A pamphlet was published reprinting articles on the strike written in the *Glasgow Socialist* by the Left socialist Selma Sigerson and copies were sent to the conference delegates. At the Drogheda conference, the national executive's main aim was to discredit Daly and to keep power out of the hands of the advanced socialists. Daly's support at the conference came mainly from his colleagues on the Dublin trades council. His main hope for success had been the achievement of a Limerick delegation that was strongly critical of the executive for its handling of the strike.

The almost unanimous vote of approval for the executive's actions over Limerick signalled a major defeat for Daly and his followers and it was the beginning of the end of his influence at the centre of the trade union movement.

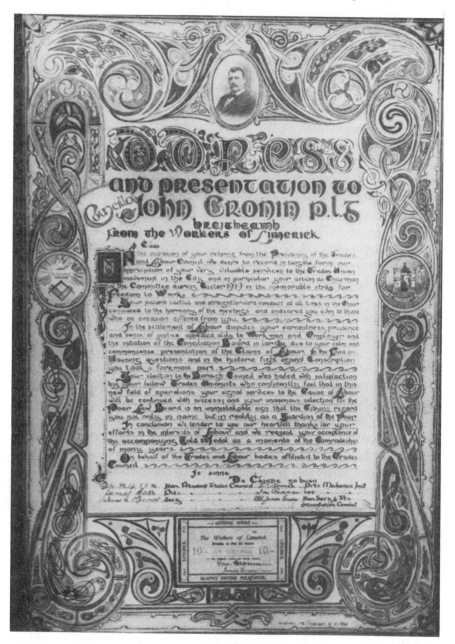

An illuminated address presented to Councillor John Cronin, Poor Law Guardian, by the workers of Limerick, marking his retirement as president of the trades council and recalling his leading role in the general strike.

Although often described as a "soviet", to what extent were the Limerick events influenced by similar happenings in Russia and the Central European countries? Some advanced Irish Labour leaders had frequently expressed approval and support for Bolshevik Russia and the soviets. For example, on the day the Limerick strike began, at a meeting of the Socialist Party of Ireland, in Dublin, Cathal O'Shannon said that the trade unions and the agricultural workers might be made the machinery through which soviets would be established in Ireland. The SPI included congress leaders like Johnson and O'Brien among its members.

At a Sinn Féin meeting in Bray, Co. Wicklow, towards the end of the soviet, the radical leader Countess Markievicz, said that if the American President Wilson failed, they had another solution — the Bolshevist revolution in Russia. The Countess, who fought in the 1916 rising in Connolly's Citizen Army, said she knew Russia well, and the people who had got control there were the rank-and-file, just as those listening to her were working and striving to earn a living and to help build up their country. They were building up a workers' Republic. That flame was sweeping westward. If it fired France, it must fire England, and if it fired England, Ireland was free [applause]. The sort of Republic they wanted to build all over the world was the workers' Republic for which James Connolly died.[21]

In the same week, one of Sinn Féin's most prominent leaders, Professor Eoin MacNeill, was worried about the impression events in Ireland were making on their supporters in America. Professor MacNeill said any statements current in America that Sinn Féin was under the red flag or was Bolshevist were not made in good faith. "We Irish", MacNeill told the *Chicago Daily News*, "are neither Russian nor international. The aim of Sinn Féin is the establishment of an independent Irish Republic in which all Irish citizens shall have a proper opportunity to live. We hold that the workers have not had that opportunity and that they must get it." A limited number of Sinn Féiners believed in state socialism, Professor MacNeill said. The Chicago special correspondent concluded: "The wind behind the Irish red flag is not strong."[22]

Possibly, MacNeill was worried about the reports from Limerick of another Chicago correspondent, Ruth Russell of the *Chicago Tribune*. In her book, *What's the Matter with Ireland ?* she vividly recalls a meeting with John Cronin and the strange mixture of socialism, nationalism and Catholicism she encountered: "All the Limerick shops I passed were blinded or shuttered. In the grey light, black lines of people moved desolately up and down, not allowed to congregate and apparently not wanting to wait in homes they were weary of. A few candles flickered in windows. At the door of a river street house, I mounted gritty stone steps. A red-badged man opened the door part way. As soon as I told him I was an American journalist the suspicious look on his face vanished. With much cordiality he invited me upstairs. While he knocked on the door he bade me wait. On the invitation to come in, I entered a badly-lit room where workingmen sat at a long, black, scratched table. I was invited to sit down. 'Yes, this is a soviet,' said John Cronin, the carpenter who was father of the baby soviet. 'Why did we form it ? Why do we pit people's rule against military rule? Of course, as workers, we are against all military ... You have seen how we have thrown the crank into production ... The "kept" press is killed, but we have substituted our own paper.' He held up a small sheet which said in large letters: 'The Workers' Bulletin-Issued by the Limerick Proletariat.' 'We have, by the way,' Cronin said, 'felt the sympathy of the union men in the army sent to guard us. A whole Scots regiment had to be sent home because it was letting workers go back and forth without passes.' A few of the workers' red-badged guards came to herald the approach of the workers, and then sat down outside the hall. Saint Munchin's chapel bell struck the Angelus. The red-badged guards rose and blessed themselves ... " [23]

More than any other piece written at the time, Ruth Russell's vignette probably gives the clearest insight into the nature of the strike-soviet and the people who were involved. They had some limited knowledge of socialist theory and a fondness for its rhetoric. They felt an emotional identification with the recent stirring events in Central Europe, Bolshevik Russia and in the more distant parts of the British empire. Some of the Limerick workers were inspired by Connolly's syndicalism mixed, as his was too, with Republicanism. They could call on an active trade union organisation and rely on passive and active support from middle-class, moderate nationalists. At the same time, they maintained a respectful relationship with the Catholic clergy who were more used to a position of leading than being led, in politics as well as in religion. Above all the cities of Ireland, Limerick had the folk memory of earlier sieges in 1690 and 1691 that had parallels with the restrictions of the military barricades and provided a rich vein of rhetoric. Mixed with all of this was an emotional and humanitarian concern for the Republican hunger-strikers, the symbolism of the death and funeral of Robert Byrne – a trade unionist and an active Republican – and the maladroit provocation of the placing of the city under martial law. All of these ingredients went into the melting pot that produced the Limerick soviet. In terms of strict theory, the Limerick strike could not be described as a soviet. There was no take-over of private property, and when the coal merchants quickly asserted their property rights in the face of the strike committee's orders, the committee backed down. This absence of a challenge to the rights of private ownership also helps to explain why General Griffin felt under no pressure to intervene against the strikers' pickets. The soviet's attitude to private property was essentially pragmatic. So long as shopkeepers were willing to act under the soviet's dictates there was no practical reason to commandeer their premises. There may also have been a view that, pending the escalation of the soviet into a general strike, it was necessary to preserve a semblance of unity across economic classes so as not to alienate actual or potential middle-class Sinn Féin support.

Few, if any, Limerick workers were either socialists or syndicalists, that is, advocates of the general strike as a means to political power, except perhaps Connolly's old lieutenant John Dowling who had come to Limerick as an organiser for the ITGWU. But they belonged to a movement, one of whose founders, its leading intellectual and martyr, had imbued syndicalist influences and bequeathed them in his theoretical writings. The movement's leaders frequently indulged in syndicalist rhetoric and its constitution was clearly syndicalist-orientated, with its organic unity of Labour Party and trade union centre and the pre-eminence of industrial aims and methods over the political.

To what extent does any trade union rank-and-file subconsciously absorb the current rhetoric of their leadership? In reaching spontaneously for a general strike as their weapon, the Limerick trade union leaders were making the natural response of members of a movement with syndicalist tendencies. Syndicalism was, in large part, one of the dominant or reinforcing ideologies of the Irish Labour movement in the years immediately after 1916, the other being nationalism. To that extent, it must have had some influence on the stances taken by the trades council in calling a general strike in Limerick, and by the strike committee in seeking a national, general strike in support.

The Limerick workers had before them too the practical example of up to eight localised general strikes in other Irish towns that had preceded their action. The first such strike took place in Youghal, Co. Cork, in December 1917. The local employers' federation locked out all the unskilled workers in the town's mills, stores and workshops in response to a wage claim by the National Union of Dock Labourers. The skilled tradesmen came out in sympathy after a week and mass pickets were placed to prevent the movement of goods. Strikers and their supporters removed horses and drays from the employers' yards and there were clashes with the RIC. After a fortnight, the strike was settled to the workers' satisfaction. In the period August 1918 to April 1919, similar local, general strikes took place in Charleville, Co. Cork; Ballina and Westport, Co. Mayo; Graiguenamanagh, Co. Kilkenny; Killarney, Co. Kerry; Boyle, Co. Roscommon; Thurles, Co. Tipperary. None of these, of course, attained the degree of organisation of the Limerick strike but they were examples of what could be achieved by united action.

Apart from the Limerick strike, 1919 was the high watermark of the syndicalist influence on Irish trade unions for another reason. The Trade Union Congress of that year adopted a re-organisation plan that involved the establishment of ten major industrial unions, all merging into the syndicalist ideal of one big union. But the plan was, effectively, shelved. It impinged too much on the autonomy of the existing trades unions, they found it hard to overcome craft and non-craft divisions and the rapidly-growing ITGWU, which saw itself as the real one big union, was hardly going to cede that position to a new, untried entity. In addition, influential leaders like Tom Johnson began the long push towards the eventual separation of the Congress from the Labour Party and the concentration on more conventional forms of organisation. Other than a contribution to trade union folklore, the Limerick general strike left little mark on trade unionism or politics in the city. The strike treasurer, James Casey, became mayor of Limerick for a short time in 1921 after British forces murdered the mayor, George Clancy, and the former mayor, Michael O'Callaghan. Casey remained a lifelong member of the Labour Party and served as a city councillor for more than twenty years. The rail workers' leader, Michael Keyes, went on to become a Labour Party Dáil deputy and held ministerial positions in the two inter-party governments formed in 1948 and 1954. In the 1930s, Keyes and Dan Clancy spoke from platforms in Limerick in support of the pro-Franco Irish Christian Front. Other leaders of the strike divided on the Anglo-Irish Treaty of 1921 and drifted away from independent working-class politics.

More importantly, the strike had no lasting influence on the Irish Labour movement nationally nor did it become a model to be followed in later phases of the War of Independence. The annual congress of 1919 urged trade unions to organise workers' councils in all cities and towns, but to little effect. There were further general strikes and there were scores of local strikes and occupations of creameries and factories – especially in the province of Munster – that were known as "soviets". In the case of the general strikes, these were purely ancillary to the Republican struggle and in no way did Labour challenge for leadership, as it did in Limerick. The occupations or soviets were too localised and too isolated to offer any concerted challenge to British rule or to the established economic and social order.

After Labour's capitulation over Limerick, the struggle for national independence was largely left up to the farming and middle classes. Labour intervened, using the strike weapon, only on occasions when it seemed Britain had overlooked the requirements of democracy or humanitarianism. But, on each occasion, the Labour leadership followed the pattern they had set in Limerick and were careful to ensure the protests did not escalate into a major political challenge, either to Britain or to the nascent Republic.

The Labour Party and Trade Union Congress that faced decisions on the later soviets was substantially different to the movement that went almost to the brink of revolution in Limerick in April 1919. Although the post-1916 Labour movement was syndicalist in organisation and rhetoric, key leaders like Tom Johnson hankered after parliamentary means to promote their policies, while others like William O'Brien applied the bulk of their energies to trade union bureaucracy and organisation. Through his participation and death in the Rising of 1916,

James Connolly, in a sense, had earned a place for Labour in the forefront of the struggle for Irish independence. Ironically, however, the executions that followed the Rising removed Connolly and other socially radical Republican leaders like Eamonn Ceannt and Sean MacDermott. In both the Labour and militant nationalist movements, leadership passed to the second rank – less courageous and more conservative in their political and social aims than those who had died.

The ITGWU remained the most practical manifestation of Connolly's syndicalist legacy to the working-class. But the trade union emphasis on syndicalism reflected the failure to develop and maintain a revolutionary political party. In this weakness, however, lay a paradoxical strength. Syndicalism emphasised rank-and-file power and decried bureaucratic officialdom. It raised the sympathetic strike and respect for the picket line into formidable weapons and it offered a form of working-class democracy, based on direct workshop representation, that seemed a plausible alternative to respectable politics. In the end, though, it could not survive the traumas of Connolly's death and Larkin's absence in America, nor the cautious leadership of their successors, Johnson and O'Brien.

As treasurer of the ITGWU, William O'Brien saw his role as one of creating the organisation to fight struggles, rather than one of leading them. But, after the high point of 1919, the union went into a long decline of membership and influence that did not stop until the growth of industrial employment nurtured by the Fianna Fáil protectionist economic policies of the 1930s. In March 1919, the ITGWU had twenty-one full-time organisers. That number stood at seventeen in May 1920, declining to eleven a year later, and by 1922 there were only nine. The union's membership fell accordingly.

Between them, O'Brien and Johnson formed the new, full-time leadership of congress with Johnson's newly-formed secretariat carrying out research and drafting policy documents. The limited administrative and political abilities of others on the congress executive gave Johnson a strong influence over policy formulation.

Johnson was a member of the Socialist Party of Ireland, but in his personal politics, his leanings were more towards trade union action rather than radical political action. But he was a conscientious listener to, and reflector of, rank-and-file views. For much of this period, he followed, rather than led trade union opinion. That explains why on so many occasions — the Limerick strike being a good example — Johnson developed the knack of sounding radical while actually restraining action. As Emmet O'Connor perceptively notes, in his work *Syndicalism in Ireland 1917-23*, "He was particularly adept at citing radical reasons for conservative decisions." [24]

By participating in the Free State Dáil of 1922, Labour, in effect, accepted the terms of the Anglo-Irish Treaty that had led to the bitter civil war. Its entry into the Dáil left it free to abandon much of its syndicalist trappings and take on the parliamentary role Johnson coveted. In doing so, it forfeited much of its rank-and-file militancy and support.

In relation to the Limerick strike of April 1919, it could be argued that it was largely the lip-service paid to syndicalism in the leadership of the Trade Union Congress that eventually led to the soviet's demise. In the end, the soviet was basically an emotional and spontaneous protest on essentially nationalist and humanitarian grounds, rather than anything based on socialist or even trade union aims.

Yet, in challenging the imposition of a special military area (SMA), the strikers were, unwittingly, striking at the root of Britain's power in Ireland. The SMAs were central to the army's strategy in their war against sedition and lawlessness. The theory of the SMAs was that the pressure and inconvenience caused to peaceful citizens would force them to give up the members of the "murder gangs in their midst". Later in the Anglo-Irish War, entire counties and regions were proclaimed under the same regulations. The right to impose military restrictions like the permit system, went to the root of British sovereignty and was crucial to plans to hold Ireland. Indeed, any denial of the right to impose such restrictions amounted to a denial of British sovereignty over Ireland.

For those reasons, the army and the RIC were pleased with the outcome of the confrontation. The strike had been called off at the intervention of a Sinn Féin mayor and a Catholic bishop who was reputed to be sympathetic to Sinn Féin. Although General Griffin had made some concessions, these were strictly compatible with the continuation of the restrictions of the special military area.

In his monthly report for April 1919, the inspector-general of the RIC enthused that the "failure of this strike is believed to have damaged the prestige of Sinn Féin with the workers".[25] The chief secretary for Ireland, MacPherson, was able to claim that the government had no hesitation in using the forces at its disposal against the strike "when Labour attempted in Limerick to use that legitimate weapon for other than industrial means – namely for unconstitutional and political ends".[26] "After the first excesses at Limerick, Belfast and Dublin", MacPherson wrote, "things were at last becoming normal and confidence was returning to the loyal, though terrorised, people." In its annual report for 1919, the Irish TUC dismissed MacPherson's comments as "a lying boast".[27]

But the strike and its ending provided little longterm encouragement for Dublin Castle. Faced early on with a choice between condemning the death of Constable O'Brien or that of Robert Byrne, "moderate" opinion in Limerick had opted for the latter. In the end, when "moderation" reasserted itself in Limerick, it was not directed against nationalism as such, but against the local and national trade union leadership involved in the strike. The initial widespread local support, and the length of the strike, should have warned the authorities that support for separatism had achieved a new, and wider, respectability. The Limerick strike was a clear warning that many elements in the civilian population were disaffected enough to provide the silent support that the Volunteers needed to launch their guerrilla war.

Despite the claims and boasts made at the ILPTUC in Drogheda, the Limerick soviet could hardly be described as a success. Mainly under clerical pressure, but also because it lacked widespread national trade union support, the strike began to fizzle out after ten days. At least the leaders adroitly turned this into an orderly, partial return to work and followed it up with a clear-cut decision some days later for a full resumption of work. In that sense, they preserved intact the machinery and morale of the Limerick trade unions, and lessened the potential for recriminations. But the Limerick strike did not dissuade the British authorities from proclaiming martial law on a wide scale in Ireland in the later period of the Anglo-Irish war. None of this is to detract from the courage, enthusiasm and remarkable organisational qualities of the strikers, which are repeatedly commented on in contemporary reports.

For three years after Easter 1916, rank-and-file militancy on issues like conscription had ensured that Labour maintained a place at the centre of the Irish struggle for independence, despite the reservations of its leadership. Until the outcome of the Limerick soviet was determined, the possibility of Labour asserting a greater leadership role still existed. The defeat of Limerick changed all that. From then on, Labour's role in the struggle for independence diminished from joint partnership to a subsidiary place. The outcome of the Limerick strike clearly determined and expressed Labour's subordination to "nation" from that point onwards.

From early in 1919, violence was emerging again as a significant factor in Irish politics. The sweeping victory of Sinn Féin in the December 1918 general election, and the establishment of the separatist Dáil Eireann in January 1919, were followed by an increasing level of violence. As Emil Strauss aptly commented in his book *Irish Nationalism and British Democracy*: "The Irish War, which began practically at the same time as the First Dáil, was to some extent a conscious assertion of leadership by the extremists." [28] In the heat of a violent war, a strike – even a general strike – seemed timid and ineffective by comparison. Nor was it a strategy that appealed to the farmers and business classes who were coming to dominate the independence movement. The result of the Limerick strike suggested to many that if political gains were to be made, sterner weapons than the strike placard would have to be used. To use a modern analogy, Labour had fulfilled its role as a booster rocket to the vehicle of mainstream nationalism. From this point onwards, when trade unionists played a part in the struggle, it was primarily in their capacity as individual members of the IRA, the IRB or the Dáil.

Had the Limerick strike achieved some success against the government, the subsequent independence struggle might have been entirely different in character. Sinn Féin and the IRA would have had to listen more closely to the economic demands of Labour and take account of them in any settlement with Britain. From such a position, Labour would have found greater support, and exerted greater influence, in the fledgeling Irish Free State. As it was, the movement never recovered politically from being perceived as remaining on the sidelines during the Anglo-Irish War and the Irish Civil War, and that political weakness has persisted to the present time.

During the years 1916 to 1923 in Ireland, therefore, the events of April 1919 in Limerick city were pivotal.

Chronology of Events

1919

13 January: Robert Byrne, trade union activist and Adjutant of Second Battalion, Limerick Brigade, Irish Republican Army (IRA) is arrested and charged with possession of a revolver and ammunition.

2-4 February: Byrne is court-martialled and sentenced to twelve months' imprisonment with hard labour. Within days, as senior officer in the prison, Byrne leads a campaign for disobedience in support of political status for IRA prisoners.

8 February: A leaflet is distributed anonymously attacking forcible feeding of Republican prisoners in Limerick Prison.

14 February: Limerick United Trades and Labour Council supports political status for the prisoners and condemns their treatment.

6-8 March: Robert Byrne is confined to bed in the prison hospital.

12 March: A weakened Byrne is removed to Number One ward of Limerick Workhouse, also known as the Union Infirmary.

Sunday, 6 April: Robert Byrne is fatally wounded during an IRA rescue at Limerick Workhouse Hospital. He dies later that evening in John Ryan's cottage in Meelick, Co. Clare.

Tuesday, 8 April: At Meelick, Co. Clare, the inquest opens into the death of Robert Byrne. His body lies in state in Limerick's pro-Cathedral.

Wednesday, 9 April: An official communiqué warns that the government will not tolerate a military parade or assembly in military formation at Byrne's funeral. Under the Defence of the Realm Acts, Brigadier General C.J.Griffin is appointed the Competent Military Authority throughout Ireland. In a separate notice, Limerick city and a part of the county is to be placed under Griffin's authority as a Special Military Area.

Thursday, 10 April: Thousands of Volunteers march in Robert Byrne's funeral to Mount Saint Laurence's Cemetery in Limerick, through streets lined by military and police.

Friday, 11 April: Limerick United Trades and Labour Council describes Robert Byrne's death as "murder" and passes a vote of condolence.

Sunday, 13 April (Palm Sunday): Limerick United Trades and Labour Council declares a general strike against the imposition of martial law.

Monday, 14 April: The military restrictions requiring workers to display special passes on their way to and from work come into effect. At five o'clock that morning, 14,000 Limerick workers begin a general strike. Gradually, the strikers tighten their control over food supplies, transport and communications.

Tuesday, 15 April: Legal representatives of Byrne's family claim his detention was illegal, and his death in custody was therefore unlawful. In Dublin executive members of the Irish Labour Party and Trade Union Congress consider the Limerick developments informally.

Wednesday, 16 April: The Catholic bishop, Dr Hallinan, and senior clergy severely criticise the military restrictions. The ILPTUC treasurer, Tom Johnson, arrives in the city. A delegation of Limerick rail workers seeking support in Dublin receives a lukewarm reception.

Thursday, 17 April: General Griffin meets Limerick Chamber of Commerce and offers to allow employers to issue permits directly to their workers. The strikers reject this concession, despite pressure from the employers. In Dublin, after three days of meetings with representatives of the separatist Dáil Eireann, the executive of the ILPTUC decides to travel to Limerick after Easter with a secret plan to evacuate the city.

Saturday, 19 April: A general meeting of prominent Limerick citizens protests against the military restrictions.

Easter Sunday, 20 April: About 1,000 young men and women gather at Caherdavin Heights and later challenge the military sentries at the boundary of the special military area.

Easter Monday, 21 April: The Caherdavin demonstrators breach the military cordon.

Tuesday, 22 April: Leaders of major British-based unions declare their opposition to the Limerick strike.

Wednesday, 23 April: Four members of the ILPTUC executive arrive in Limerick. They immediately begin a continuous series of meetings with the local strike leaders, who are under the impression that a national strike is to be called. They reject the ILPTUC plan for a protest evacuation.

Thursday, 24 April: Mediation by the Catholic bishop, Dr Hallinan, and the Sinn

Féin mayor, Alphonsus O'Mara, produces a peace formula. A strike committee proclamation allows all workers who can get to their work without passing military barricades to resume work immediately.

Friday, 25 April: Most of the strikers resume work. Only those requiring military permits remain out.

Saturday, 26 April: Some residents of Thomondgate – still cut off from work by the military barricades – block Thomondgate bridge in protest.

Sunday, 27 April: A strike committee proclamation calls for a full resumption of work.

Monday, 28 April: The remaining strikers resume work. Limerick United Trades and Labour Council decides not to take part in a May Day stoppage.

5 May: The military restrictions on Limerick are officially ended.

References

Chapter 1
The Empires Crumble

1 *Irish Independent*, 15.4.1919
2 *The Irish Times*, 7.4.1919
3 *The Irish Times*, 8.4.1919
4 Mitchell, David, "Ghost of a Chance: British Revolutionaries in 1919", in *History Today*, Vol. XX, No.11, November 1970, pp.753-761
5 ILPTUC Annual Report 1919, p.18
6 ITGWU Annual Report 1918, p.8
7 ITGWU Annual Report 1918, p.7
8 ITGWU, Cathal O'Shannon (Ed.), *Fifty Years of Liberty Hall*, 1959, pp.72,73
9 ITGWU, *The Lines of Progress*, 1918
10 ILPTUC Annual Report 1919, p.19
11 Fox, R.M., *Labour in the National Struggle*, p.10; MacCann, Sean,*War by the Irish*, 1946, p.78
12 MacCann, Sean, *War by the Irish*, pp.78,79
13 ILPTUC Annual Report 1919, p.19
14 ILPTUC Annual Report 1919, p.19
15 Fox, R.M., *Labour in the National Struggle*, p.9
16 ibid p.9
17 ibid p.10
18 ibid p.10
19 " Memorandum to Mansion House Conference", no date, Tom Johnson papers, National Library of Ireland (NLI) MS. 17115
20 Public Record Office (PRO), Cab 23, W O Series, 21.11.1918
21 Count Plunkett papers, NLI, MS.11405
22 PRO, CO 904 108 Monthly Report Inspector-General (I-G) Royal Irish Constabulary (RIC), February 1919

23 Fox, R.M., *Labour in the National Struggle*, pp.14,15
24 *The Irish Times*, 8.4.1919
25 *Irish Independent*, 22.4.1919
26 *Irish Independent*, 10.4.1919

Chapter 2
Connolly's Legacy

1 Annual Report I-G RIC, 1918
2 PRO, CO 904 108 Monthly Report I-G RIC, March 1919
3 Cited in R.M.Fox, *Labour in the National Struggle*,
4 *Irish Worker*, 30.5.1914
5 Connolly, James, *Labour in Irish History*, cited in Fox, R.M., *Labour in the National Struggle*, p.6
6 *The Workers' Republic*, 22.1.1916
7 Fox, R.M., *Labour in the National Struggle*, p.3
8 Ryan, W.P., *The Irish Labour Movement*, p.326
9 *The Times*, 22,23.1.1919
10 *Daily News*, 22.1.1919
11 Townsend, Charles, *The British Campaign in Ireland 1919-21*, p.15
12 Molan, Timothy, *The Limerick Soviet*, p.62
13 Fox, R.M., *Labour in the National Struggle*, p.19; Farrell, Brian, *The Founding of Dáil Eireann*, Appendix
14 Breen, Dan, *My Fight for Irish Freedom*, 1924, pp.32,33
15 Townsend, Charles, *The British Campaign in Ireland 1919-21*, p.1
16 PRO, GT 6574 CAB 2472/1

Chapter 3
Limerick, A Defiant City

1 *The Times*, 17.3.1913, Irish Supplement
2 Limerick United Trades and Labour Council (LUTLC) Minute book 11.2.1916
3 Kemmy, Jim, "The Limerick Soviet", in *Saothar 2*, Journal of the Irish Labour History Society, p.45
4 ITUCLP Annual Report, 1914
5 *The Bottom Dog*, 20.10.1917
6 *The Bottom Dog*, 3.11.1917
7 LUTLC *Minute Book*, May 1918
8 ibid, May 1918
9 ibid, May 1918
10 ibid, May 1918
11 *The Soldier Hunter*, 23.2.1918
12 Kemmy, Jim, "The Limerick Soviet" ,in *Saothar 2*, p.46; Ed. McCarthy, J.M., *Limerick's Fighting Story*, p.178
13 *The Soldier Hunter*, 23.2.1918
14 ibid, 23.2.1918
15 ibid, 23.2.1918
16 Military Intelligence Special Division report, February 1917
17 Molan, Timothy, *The Limerick Soviet*, p.96

Chapter 4
Robert Byrne, A Republican Trade Unionist

1 *The Irish Times*, 7.4.1919; *Irish Independent*, 7.4.1919
2 State Paper Office (SPO), CBS Papers, Carton 23
3 SPO, CBS Papers, Green File 17
4 *Irish Independent*, 8.4.1919
5 *The Bottom Dog*, 2.2.1919
6 PRO, CO 904 167
7 *Irish Independent*, 2.1.1919
8 ibid, 2.1.1919
9 ibid, 2.1.1919
10 PRO, CO 904 167

11 SPO, Chief Secretary's Office Registered Papers (CSORP), 1919, 1354, 3489, 3783, 5672, 4331
12 SPO, CSORP, 1919, 3809
13 ibid, 3809
14 SPO, CSORP, 1919, 4244
15 ibid, 4244
16 *Limerick Leader*, 13.2.1919; *The Irish Times*, 14.2.1919
17 SPO, CSORP, 1919, 4559
18 SPO, CSORP, 1919, 5304
19 SPO, CSORP, 1919, 9537, 31044
20 PRO, CO 904 167
21 LUTLC Minute Book, 14.2.1919
22 *Limerick's Fighting Story*, p.179
23 *The Irish Times*, 8.4.1919; *Irish Independent*, 8.4.1919
24 *The Irish Times*, 8.4.1919; *Irish Independent*, 8.4.1919
25 SPO, CSORP 1919, 9501 (Changed to 24267/S/1919); 10482 (Changed to 24267/S/1919); 10893
26 SPO, CSORP, 1919, 9529
27 LUTLC Minute Book, 11.4.1919
28 ibid, 11.4.1919
29 LUTLC Minute Book, May 1919 (contains the original letter)

Chapter 5
Funeral and Inquest

1 SPO, CSORP, 1919, 11796
2 *Irish Independent*, 10.4.1919
3 *Irish Independent*, 11.4.1919
4 *Irish Independent*, 16.4.1919; *The Irish Times*, 16.4.1919
5 SPO, CSORP, 1919, 11397
6 *Irish Independent*, 17.4.1919
7 ibid, 17.4.1919
8 SPO, CSORP, 1919, 10115
9 *Irish Independent*, 17.4.1919
10 Stack, Michael "Batty", interview with Jim Kemmy; St George, Charles, interview with Kevin O'Connor, 1988

Chapter 6
Soldiers and Strikers

1 PRO, WO 32 62
2 Dalgleish, James, "The Limerick General Strike 1919", Appendix 2
3 *The Irish Times*, 8.4.1919; *Irish Independent*, 8.4.1919
4 PRO, CO 904 187
5 *The Irish Times*, 9.9.1919
6 Dalgleish, James, "The Limerick General Strike 1919", p.123
7 District-Inspector (D-I) RIC Monthly Report, April 1919, PRO CO 904 108
8 *Irish Independent*, 15.4.1919
9 *The Irish Times*, 15.4.1919
10 *Irish Independent*, 15.4.1919
11 *The Irish Times*, 15.4.1919
12 *Irish Independent*, 15.4.1919
13 *Irish Independent*, *The Irish Times*, 15.4.1919
14 SPO, CSORP, 1919, 9813
15 ibid, 9813
16 ibid, 9813
17 ibid, 9813
18 ibid, 9813
19 ibid, 9813
20 ibid, 9813
21 ibid, 9813
22 SPO, CSORP, 1919, 10147
23 SPO, CSORP, 1919, 10042
24 SPO, CSORP, 1919, 9839; 10683
25 SPO, CSORP, 1919, 10411
26 *Irish Independent*, 10.4.1919
27 SPO, CSORP, 1919, 11611
28 SPO, CSORP, 1919, 15113
29 *Irish Independent*, 8.2.1919; SPO, CSORP, 1919, 15113
30 *Irish Independent*, *The Irish Times*, 21.4.1919; SPO, CSORP, 10390

Chapter 7
Food, Money and Newspapers

1 *Irish Independent*, 16.4.1919

2 *The Irish Times*, 15.4.1919
3 *The Irish Times*, 15.4.1919
4 *Irish Independent*, 16.4.1919
5 *Irish Independent*, 23.4.1919
6 *Irish Independent*, 26.4.1919
7 *Irish Independent*, *The Irish Times*, 21.4.1919
8 *Irish Independent*, 17.4.1919, *The Irish Times*, 19.4.1919
9 *Irish Independent*, 21.4.1919
10 *The Irish Times*, 21.4.1919
11 *Irish Independent*, 22.4.1919
12 *The Irish Times*, 22.4.1919
13 *Irish Independent*, 17.4.1919
14 SPO, CSORP, 1919, 10768
15 *Limerick Socialist*, April 1972, p.4
16 *The Irish Times*, 24.4.1919
17 *Limerick's Fighting Story*, p.190; Kemmy, Jim, "The Limerick Soviet", *The Irish Times*, 9.5.1969
18 O'Connor, Kevin, "The Limerick Soviet", RTE radio documentary, transcript p.26
19 *Irish Independent*, 17.4.1919
20 *The Irish Times*, 21.4.1919
21 *Irish Independent*, 22.4.1919
22 *Irish Independent*, 22.4.1919
23 *The Irish Times*, 23.4.1919
24 *Limerick's Fighting Story*, p.189
25 *Irish Independent*, 19.4.1919
26 *Limerick's Fighting Story*, p.189
27 *Limerick's Fighting Story*, p.190-91
28 *Irish Independent*, 24.4.1919

Chapter 8
The World Watches

1 *The Irish Times*, 7.4.1919
2 *Irish Independent*, 16.4.1919, 19.4.1919; *The Irish Times*, 16.4.1919
3 Reported in *The Irish Times*, 16.4.1919
4 *Irish Independent*, 21.4.1919
5 *The Irish Times*, 19.4.1919
6 Reported in *Irish Independent*, 25.4.1919

7 Reported in *Irish Independent*,
  25.4.1919
8 Reported in *Irish Independent*,
  24.4.1919
9 Reported in *Irish Independent*,
  23.4.1919
10 Reported in *Irish Independent*,
  24.4.1919
11 Reported in *The Irish Times*, 22.4.1919
12 Reported in *Irish Independent*,
  22.4.1919
13 Reported in *Irish Independent*,
  23.4.1919
14 Reported in *Irish Independent*,
  23.4.1919
15 Reported in *Irish Independent*,
  23.4.1919
16 Reported in *Irish Independent*,
  26.4.1919
17 *Irish Independent*, 23.4.1919
18 *The Irish Times*, 7.4.1919
19 *The Irish Times*, 15.4.1919
20 *The Irish Times*, 23.4.1919

Chapter 9
Confrontation

1 *The Irish Times, Irish Independent*,
  19.4.1919
2 *Workers' Bulletin*, 19.4.1919
3 *The Irish Times, Irish Independent*,
  19.4.1919
4 *The Irish Times, Irish Independent* ,
  22.4.1919; O'Connor, Kevin, "The
  Limerick Soviet", RTE radio documentary, transcript p.29
5 *The Irish Times*, 22.4.1919
6 *Munster News*, 26.4.1919
7 *The Irish Times*, 23.4.1919
8 *Workers' Bulletin*, 23.4.1919
9 *Workers' Bulletin*, 21.4.1919
10 *Workers' Bulletin*, 21.4.1919,
  23.4.1919
11 *Workers' Bulletin*, 21.4.1919
12 *The Irish Times*, 19.4.1919
13 *Workers' Bulletin*, 18.4.1919

14 Cited in *Limerick's Fighting Story*, p.18
15 *Limerick's Fighting Story*, p.18
16 *Irish Independent*, 22.4.1919
17 *The Irish Times*, 17.4.1919; *Irish Independent*, 17.4.1919

Chapter 10
Bosses and Clergy

1 SPO, CSORP, 1919, 10918
2 *The Irish Times, Irish Independent*,
  21.4.1919
3 ibid, 21.4.1919
4 ibid, 21.4.1919
5 ibid, 21.4.1919
6 ibid, 21.4.1919; SPO, CSORP, 1919,
  10390
7 SPO, CSORP, 1919, 10390
8 SPO, CSORP, 1919, 18692
9 *Irish Independent*, 17.4.1919
10 *Limerick's Fighting Story*, p.192
11 *The Irish Times*, 17.4.1919
12 *Workers' Bulletin*, 21.4.1919
13 *The Irish Times*, 15.4.1919
14 Reported in *Irish Independent*, 3.5.1919

Chapter 11
The Workers Defeated

1 *Irish Independent*, 16.4.1919
2 *Workers' Bulletin*, 23.4.1919
3 *Irish Independent*, 16.4.1919
4 ILPTUC Annual Report 1919, p.78
5 *Irish Independent*, 19.4.1919
6 ibid, 19.4.1919
7 *The Irish Times*, 23.4.1919
8 SPO, CSORP, 1919, 10926
9 *Irish Independent*, 17.4.1919
10 *Irish Independent*, 19.4.1919
11 *Irish Independent*, 23.4.1919
12 *Irish Independent*, 22.4.1919
13 *The Irish Times*, 23.4.1919
14 *Munster News*, 26.4.1919
15 *The Irish Times, Irish Independent*,
  25.4.1919

16 *Munster News*, 26.4.1919; Kemmy, Jim, *Saothar 2*, p.51

17 *The Irish Times*, 26.4.1919

18 *The Irish Times, Irish Independent*, 25.4.1919

19 *The Irish Times, Irish Independent*, 25.4.1919

20 *The Irish Times, Irish Independent*, 25.4.1919

21 *Irish Independent*, 26.4.1919

22 *The Irish Times*, 26.4.1919

23 *The Irish Times, Irish Independent*, 28.4.1919

Chapter 12
Green, Red and Orange

1 *The Irish Times, Irish Independent*, 26.4.1919

2 *Limerick Leader*, 12.5.1919; *Limerick Chronicle*, cited in Kemmy, Jim, *Saothar 2*, p.51

3 *Irish Independent*, 26.4.1919

4 ibid, 26.4.1919

5 *The Irish Times*, 23.4.1919

6 Kemmy, Jim, "Women and the Limerick Soviet", *Limerick Socialist*, May 1979, pp.4-6

7 *Irish Independent*, 24.4.1919

8 *Irish Independent*, 25.4.1919

9 SPO, CSORP, 1919, 10897

10 SPO, CSORP, 1919, 10734

11 SPO, CSORP, 1919, 11202

12 SPO, CSORP, 1919, 11201

13 SPO, CSORP, 1919, 11203

14 Reported in *Irish Independent*, 23.4.1919

15 *Irish Independent*, 26.4.1919

16 ibid, 26.4.1919

17 ibid, 26.4.1919

18 ibid, 26.4.1919

19 ibid, 26.4.1919

20 ibid, 26.4.1919

21 ibid, 28.4.1919

22 ibid, 28.4.1919

23 ibid, 28.4.1919

24 LUTLC Minute Book, 28.4.1919

25 *Irish Independent*, 5.5.1919

Epilogue

1 ILPTUC Annual Report 1919, pp.56-58, 73-83

2 ILPTUC Annual Report 1919, p.73

3 ILPTUC Annual Report 1919, p.76

4 ILPTUC Annual Report 1919, p.77

5 ILPTUC Annual Report 1919, p.78

6 ILPTUC Annual Report 1919, p.80

7 ILPTUC Annual Report 1919, p.80

8 ILPTUC Annual Report 1919, pp.81, 82

9 ILPTUC Annual Report 1919, p.83

10 *New Statesman*, 4.12.1920

11 *Freeman's Journal*, 23.4.1919; *Munster News*, 26.4.1919

12 *The Irish Times*, 21.4.1919

13 Reported in *Irish Independent*, 28.4.1919

14 *New Ireland*, 3.5.1919; Kemmy, Jim, "The Limerick Soviet", *Saothar 2*, p.52

15 *The Irish Times*, 23.4.1919

16 *An Phoblacht*, (The Republic), 3.5.1919

17 *An tEireannach*, (The Irishman), 3.5.1919

18 *Dublin Saturday Post*, 10.5.1919

19 *Dublin Saturday Post*, 17.5.1919

20 LUTLC Minute Book, 25.7.1919

21 *Irish Independent*, 26.4.1919

22 ibid, 26.4.1919

23 Russell, Ruth, *What's the Matter with Ireland*, cited in Kemmy, Jim, *Saothar 2*, p. 50

24 O'Connor, Emmet, *Syndicalism in Ireland 1917-23*, Cork 1988, p.66

25 PRO, CO 904 108 I-G RIC Monthly report for April 1919

26 *Irish Independent*, 30.4.1919, and Strathcarron Papers, Bodleian Library Oxford

27 ILPTUC Annual Report 1919, p.58

28 Strauss, Emil, *Irish Nationalism and British Democracy*, London 1951

Sources

Official Records
State Paper Office, Dublin Castle (SPO):
Chief Secretary's Office Registered Papers 1918-20 inclusive
General Prisons Board Papers 1917-20 inclusive
Public Record Office, London (PRO):
CO 903 19 5 Intelligence Notes, Chief Secretary's Office, Judicial Division
CO 904 20 United Irish League
CO 904 39 Judicial Proceedings 1918-21
CO 904 108/109 Inspector-General RIC, Confidential Reports on Limerick
CO 904 158 4 Strikes, 1918-19
CO 904 161 4 Seizures of leaflets, postcards etc. 1915-19
CO 904 164 Mail, correspondence 1916
CO 904 167 2 Press Censor's Reports Jan-Mar 1919
CO 904 169 1 DORA Custody of Persons Awaiting Trial
CO 904 169 2 Prohibition of meetings 1918-20
CO 904 169 3 Orders by Competent Military Authorities
CO 904 177 1 Attempted murder of constables
CO 904 187 1 Withdrawals of Troops 1917-19
CO 906 18 Treatment of Internees 1918-19
WO 35 69 6 Publication of Seditious Articles 1916-20
WO 35 172 Movement of Troops in Ireland 1919-21 (Retained by War Office)
WO 35 173 Royal Flying Corps in Ireland 1917-19 (Retained by War Office)
WO 182 Part 1/1/2 Record of Hostilities and Events 1919-21

Trade Union Records
Limerick United Trades and Labour Council (LUTLC) Minute Book 22.3.1918-
    September 1920
Irish Labour Party and Trade Union Congress (ILPTUC) Annual Report 1919
"Ireland at Berne", Report ILPTUC 1919
National Union of Railwaymen (NUR) Executive Committee Minute Book 1919

Newspapers
The Irish Times, Jan-May 1919
Irish Independent, Jan-May 1919
Limerick Leader, Mar-May 1919
Munster News and Clare Advocate, Limerick, April 1919
Weekly Observer, Newcastle West, Co. Limerick, April 1919

The Bottom Dog, Limerick, Oct 1917-Aug 1918
The Workers' Bulletin, Limerick, April 1919
Watchdog, Limerick, Nov. 1919
Workers' Bulletin, Belfast, April 1919
Red Flag, Dublin, Nov. 1919
Le Matin, Paris, April-May 1919

BIBLIOGRAPHY

THE LIMERICK SOVIET

Breen, John, "A Flame in the Spring — the Story of the Limerick Soviet", pageant; first performance 18 April 1989, Belltable Art Centre, Limerick

Cahill, Liam, "The Limerick Soviet: The influence of Syndicalism on the Irish Labour Movement 1916-1919", lecture to Irish Labour History Society, October 1979, and to Waterford Labour History Society, December 1981

Cahill, Liam, "The Limerick Soviet: Sixty Years On", article, *Civil Service Review*, July/August 1979

Cahill, Liam, "Brief Life of the Limerick Soviet", article, *Irish Independent*, 17 April 1979

Cahill, Liam, "Cathair Luimní faoi smacht Coiste Stailce", article, *Irish Press*, 7 April 1979

Cahill Liam, "The Limerick Soviet 1919: Its Place in History and Politics", 70th Anniversary Commemorative Lecture, Limerick, April 14 1989

Casey, James, "A Limerick Challenge to British Tyranny" chapter in *Limerick's Fighting Story*, pp.185 et. seq.

Cross, Brian, "Limerick Soviet Commemorative Show", catalogue, Limerick Municipal Gallery, 24 April to 14 May 1989

Dalgleish, James M, "The Limerick General Strike, 1919", thesis, University of Warwick, 1977

Deegan, James, "The Limerick Soviet", paper, to Irish Conference of History Students 1978

Hanamy, John, *Strike*, a play on the Limerick Soviet; first performance May Day 1989 by Pretentious Productions, Ark Tavern, Corbally

Hehir, Niamh, "The Limerick Soviet Revisited", lecture, Annual Seminar, Limerick Labour History Research Group, 16 January 1989

Hehir, Niamh, and Morrissey, Joe, "Ten Days that Shook Limerick", article, in *Revolt of the Bottom Dog*, schools history pack, Limerick Labour History Research Group, January 1989

Holmes, Eamon, "The Limerick Soviet 1919", BA mini-thesis, UCD 1977

Kemmy, Jim, "The Limerick Soviet", article, *The Irish Times*, 9 May 1969

Kemmy, Jim, "The Limerick Soviet", series of articles, *Limerick Socialist*, April 1972-February 1973

Kemmy, Jim, "The Limerick Soviet", article, *Saothar 2*, Journal of the Irish Labour Irish Society, 1975-76

Kemmy, Jim, "Women and the Limerick Soviet", *Limerick Socialist*, May 1979

Kemmy, Jim, "The General Strike 1919", article, *The Old Limerick Journal*, No. 2, March 1980

Kemmy, Jim, "The Limerick Soviet of 1919", lecture to Galway Labour History Group, June 1988

MacCann, Sean, "Limerick Accepts a Challenge", chapter in MacCann, Sean, *War by the Irish*, pp.94-98, April 1946

Molan, Timothy, "The Limerick Soviet 1919", thesis, NIHE, Limerick n.d.

O'Loughlin, Michael, "Limerick, 1919", poem, *Atlantic Blues*, Raven Arts Press, 1982

"Mystery of the Limerick Soviet Notes", article, *Irish Numismatics*, (Ed. Young, Derek), No. 16, July/August 1970

"The Limerick Soviet", supplement issued in 1985, *Liberty*, Journal of ITGWU, Diamond Jubilee Edition, 1984

O'Connor Lysaght, D.R., *The Story of the Limerick Soviet*, pamphlet, Limerick Branch of People's Democracy, 1979

O'Connor, Kevin, "The Limerick Soviet", radio documentary, RTE, June 1974

O'Connor, Kevin, *Permits Please*, play, first performance 1989

GENERAL

Books

Bowyer Bell, J., *The Secret Army*, London 1972

Boyce, D.G., *Englishmen and Irish Troubles*, London 1972

Boyce, D.G., *Nationalism in Ireland*, London 1982

Caulfield, Max, *The Easter Rebellion*, New York/London 1963

Dunsmore Clarkson, J., *Labour and Nationalism in Ireland*, New York 1926

Cody, O'Dowd, Rigny, *The Parliament of Labour: 100 Years of the Dublin Council of Trade Unions*, Dublin 1986

Comerford, Maire, *The First Dáil*, Mercier Press, Dublin.

Connolly, James, *Socialism made Easy*, Socialist Labour Press, Dublin 1918

Connolly, James, *The Reconquest of Ireland*, Dublin/Belfast 1968

Connolly-Walker Controversy, British and Irish Communist Organisation, Belfast 1969

Dawson, Richard, *Red Terror and Green*, London 1920

Donovan, T.M., *Revolution: Christian or Communist* (pamphlet *c.* 1920s)

Dwyer, T. Ryle, *Eamon de Valera*, Dublin 1980

Beresford Ellis, P., *A History of the Irish Working Class*, London 1972

Farrell, Brian, *The Founding of Dáil Eireann*, Gill and Macmillan, Dublin 1971

Fyfe, Hamilton, *Keir Hardie*, London 1935

Fitzpatrick, David, *Politics and Irish Life 1913-21*, Dublin 1977

Fox, R.M., *Labour in the National Struggle*, Irish Labour Party, Dublin 1947

Greaves, C. Desmond, *The Life and Times of James Connolly*, London 1961

Greaves, C. Desmond, *Liam Mellowes and the Irish Revolution*, London 1971

Greaves, C. Desmond, *The Irish Transport and General Workers' Union: The Formative Years*, Dublin 1982

Hepburn, A. C., *The Conflict of Nationality in Ireland*, London 1980

Holt, Edgar, *Protest in Arms: the Irish Troubles 1916-23*, New York 1961

Hunt, R. N. Carew, *The Theory and Practice of Communism*, London 1963

Inglis, Brian, *Roger Casement*, London 1974

Keogh, Dermot, *The Rise of the Irish Working Class*, Belfast 1982

Larkin, Emmet, *James Larkin: Labour Leader*, London 1965

Lawler. Sheila, *Britain and Ireland 1914-23*, Dublin 1983

Limerick Teachers' Educational Committee n.d. *Limerick: A Handbook of Local History*

Lyons, F.S.L., *Charles Stewart Parnell*, London 1977

Lysaght, D.R. O'Connor, *The Republic of Ireland*, Cork 1970

Macardle, Dorothy, *The Irish Republic*, London 1968

MacCann, Sean, *War by the Irish*, The Kerryman Ltd., Tralee 1946

McCarthy, Charles, *Trade Unions in Ireland 1894-1960*, Dublin 1977

McCarthy, J.M., (Ed.), *Limerick's Fighting Story*, Limerick n.d.

Mansergh, Nicholas, *Ireland in the Age of Reform and Revolution*,

Milotte, Mike, *Communism in Modern Ireland*, London 1984

Morgan, Austen, *James Connolly: A Political Biography*, Manchester 1988

Morgan, Austen, and Purdie, Bob, (Eds.), *Ireland: Divided Nation, Divided Class*, London 1980

Nevin, Donal, (Ed.), *Trade Unions and Change in Irish Society*, Cork 1980

O'Brien, William, (Ed. Mc Lysaght, Edward), *Forth the Banners Go*, Dublin 1969

O Broin, Leon, *Michael Collins*, Dublin 1980

O'Connor, Emmet, *Syndicalism in Ireland 1917-23*, Cork 1988

O'Malley, Ernie, *The Singing Flame*, Tralee 1978

Paul, William, *The Irish Crisis: Ireland and World Revolution*, (pamphlet) Communist Party of Great Britain, London

Ryan, W.P., *The Irish Labour Movement*, Dublin 1919

Strauss, Emil, *Irish Nationalism and British Democracy*, London 1951

Townsend, Charles, *The British Campaign in Ireland 1919-21*, Oxford University Press, 1973

Articles/pamphlets

Fitzpatrick, David, "Strikes in Ireland 1914-21", *Saothar* 6 (1980), pp.26-39

Gilmore, George, "The Relevance of James Connolly in Ireland Today", Dublin 1975

Goldring, Maurice, "Connolly Reassessed", *Saothar* 7 (1981),pp.50-53

Hamilton, Frank, "Ben Dinneen and Days of the Bottom Dog", address, 4 June 1987

Hamilton, Frank "The Bottom Dog: A Study in Irish Labour Journalism", n.d.

"Historic Limerick, the City and Its Treasures", *The Irish Heritage* Series, No.45

Hobsbawm, E.J., "Working Classes and Nations", *Saothar 8* (1982),pp.75-85

Kenny, Bob, "The Growth of the Irish Transport and General Workers' Union: A Geographer's View" *Saothar 12* (1987),pp.78-85

Lee, Joseph, "Irish Nationalism and Socialism: Rumpf Reconsidered", *Saothar 6* (1980),pp.59-64

Lenin, V.I., *Lenin on Ireland*, (pamphlet), Communist Party of Ireland, Dublin 1970

Liberty, Journal of the ITGWU, Diamond Jubilee edition 1984

Lysaght, D.R. O'Connor, "County Tipperary: class struggle and national struggle 1916-24", *Tipperary: History and Society*, Ed. William Nolan, Dublin 1985

Lysaght, D.R. O'Connor, "The Rake's Progress of a Syndicalist: The Political Career of William O'Brien, Irish Labour Leader", *Saothar 9* (1983),pp.48-63

Mac Giolla Coille, Breandan, "Mourning the Martyrs", *The Old Limerick Journal*, No.22, 1987 (Christmas edition),pp.29-44

McCarthy, Charles, "Labour and the 1922 General Election", *Saothar 7* (1981),pp.15-121

McCarthy, Terry, *Labour v Sinn Féin*, (pamphlet), National Museum of Labour History Publications, Labour Museum pamphlet No. 1

Mapstone, Richard H., "Trade Union and Government Relations: A Case Study of Influence on the Stormount Government", *Saothar 12* (1987),pp.35-46

Morgan, Austen, "A British Labourist in Catholic Ireland", *Saothar 7* (1981),pp.54-61

Newsinger, John, á'As Catholic as the Pope': James Connolly and the Roman Catholic Church in Ireland", *Saothar 11* (1986),pp.7-18

O'Connor, Emmet, "Agrarian Unrest and the Labour Movement in County Waterford, 1917-23", *Saothar 6* (1980), pp.40-58

O'Connor, Emmet, "An Age of Agitation", *Saothar 9* (1983),pp.64-71

Probert, Belinda, "Marxism and the Irish Question", *Saothar 6* (1980),pp.65-71

Purdie, Bob, "Red Hand or Red Flag? Loyalism and Workers in Belfast", *Saothar 8* (1982),pp.64-69

Saothar, Journal of the Irish Labour History Society Nos.2-13

Schneider, Fred D., "Ireland and British Labour", *The Review of Politics*, July 1978, University of Notre Dame Press

Shaw, Francis, "The Canon of Irish History — A Challenge", *Studies*, Summer 1972,pp.115-153

Other Sources

O'Brien Papers, National Library of Ireland, MS 15654 - Letters of Thomas Farren

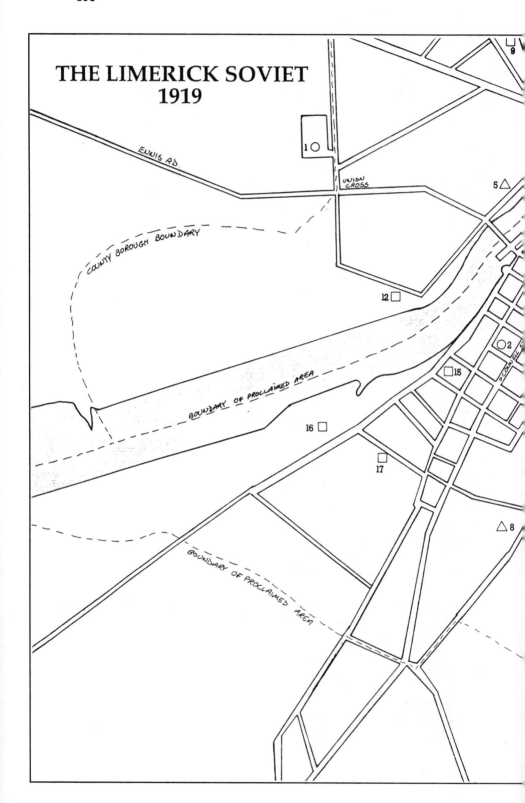

THE LIMERICK SOVIET
1919

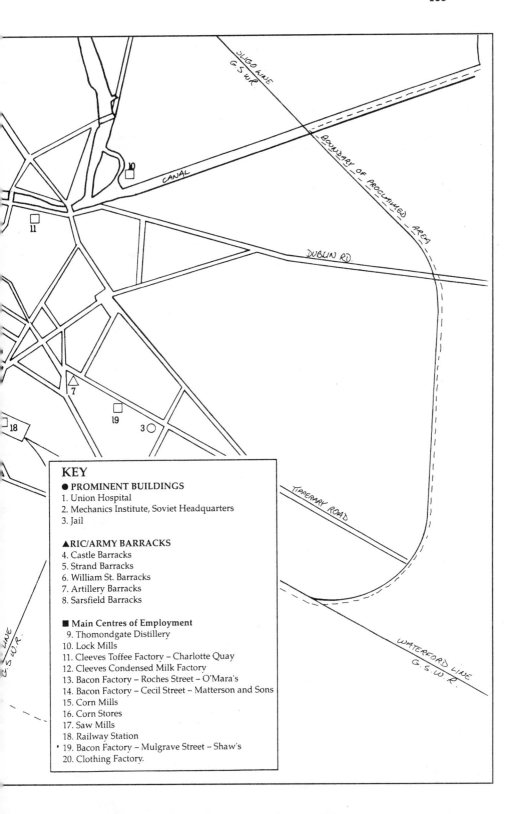

KEY

● PROMINENT BUILDINGS
1. Union Hospital
2. Mechanics Institute, Soviet Headquarters
3. Jail

▲ RIC/ARMY BARRACKS
4. Castle Barracks
5. Strand Barracks
6. William St. Barracks
7. Artillery Barracks
8. Sarsfield Barracks

■ Main Centres of Employment
9. Thomondgate Distillery
10. Lock Mills
11. Cleeves Toffee Factory – Charlotte Quay
12. Cleeves Condensed Milk Factory
13. Bacon Factory – Roches Street – O'Mara's
14. Bacon Factory – Cecil Street – Matterson and Sons
15. Corn Mills
16. Corn Stores
17. Saw Mills
18. Railway Station
19. Bacon Factory – Mulgrave Street – Shaw's
20. Clothing Factory.

INDEX